Corporate Memory

This book is dedicated to people who believe in Shooting Stars, to Jan Johannessen, Barry Stamps and believers yet to be identified.

Corporate Memory

Strategies for Knowledge Management

Annie Brooking

INTERNATIONAL THOMSON BUSINESS PRESS
I(T)P® **An International Thomson Publishing Company**

London • Bonn • Johannesburg • Madrid • Melbourne • Mexico City • New York • Paris
Singapore • Tokyo • Toronto • Albany, NY • Belmont, CA • Cincinnati, OH • Detroit, MI

Corporate Memory: Strategies for Knowledge Management

Copyright © 1999 International Thomson Business Press

I(T)P® A division of International Thomson Publishing Inc.
The ITP logo is a trademark under licence

British Library Cataloguing-in-Publication Data
A catalogue record for this book is available from the British Library

First published 1999 by International Thomson Business Press

Typeset by J&L Composition Ltd, Filey, North Yorkshire
Printed in the UK by TJ International, Padstow, Cornwall

ISBN 1–86152–268–1

International Thomson Business Press
Berkshire House
168–173 High Holborn
London WCIV 7AA
UK

http://www.itbp.com

CONTENTS

LIST OF FIGURES

LIST OF TABLES

ACKNOWLEDGEMENTS

I would like to thank those who helped me to research and write this book. First, Bill Blake COO of The Technology Broker who stepped in to run the company in order to give me time to write this book, and its sister *Dream Ticket*. Next, to the individuals at The Technology Broker who helped me to research the book, and who were my colleagues on projects which generated much of the material herein: Philip Harriss, Sue Jones, David Parker, Raj Muru and Carl Jackson. Lastly, I have to thank my personal assistant Sue (Biggsey) Biggs who diligently checked the document, and was always there to respond to my (mostly unreasonable) requests and timetables. Thanks Guys.

I'd also like to thank those who encouraged me to keep going when I set myself a silly timetable to write and launch the Intellectual Capital Series: to Susan and Peter Dennis, my mother Margaret and Neil Hitch.

Finally thank you to my editor Julian Thomas, who managed to hide his frustration with me with magnificent aplomb, even when I missed every deadline.

1

The Knowledge Based Company

Have you noticed that you might not be an employee any more – but a 'knowledge worker'? Have you wondered what you are doing differently to get this new title? Has your spouse proudly announced to the family – 'Well . . . Gerry is a knowledge worker now you know'? What's a knowledge worker anyhow? Were you a dumb worker before?

This new label, 'knowledge worker', has arisen in recent years as the result of a general consensus that knowledge in the company is a jolly important asset. How many times have you heard a manager remark – 'Our employees are our most important asset' – is that really true? Why? I can draw up an impressive list of past and present colleagues I consider to have been a huge liability. Such sayings have become commonplace in today's companies. However the saying is empty, as it's not always the people who are valuable (they may even be a liability!), but the knowledge, know-how, experience and competencies they possess are very valuable. By and large managers do not necessarily know who is valuable in the organization and who is not. Evidence of this is provided by the number of companies that have made employees redundant as a result of reengineering only to hire them back as (more expensive) consultants.

The anecdotes go on and on: a major computer services provider has developed seven document management systems in recent years – each developer thought they were the first. They also discovered they had 51 different versions of the same customer agreement! Patents filed by companies are forgotten, and reinvented. Surveys carried out by an oil company are forgotten, and a chance remark by an old employee informs management that the area was surveyed 20 years ago, saving the company millions of dollars. Companies rely on long-standing employees to act as their 'corporate memory', but when these people leave, links to the past are permanently severed.

Is the asset the people or the knowledge they possess? Funny but, like many of you, I thought we'd been knowledgeable about all sorts of things since we commenced to be alive. So why are we knowledge workers today, when we weren't before?

HINDSIGHT – A PRETTY VIEW?

If we look back towards the early 1900s and examine the nature of industry, particularly successful industries, we see smoke stack operations, where valuable commodities are machinery and the state-of-the-art factories that housed them. Employees are drones. Recall the cult silent movie *Metropolis*, made in 1926, which portrayed the future of the workplace as a human treadmill, where grey humans, too exhausted even to look up, ministered to ever hungry machines. The movie bizarrely concludes with the heroine morphing into a robot then back to being human – escaping from her machine form to the dismay of her power hungry masters. Not a surprising vision, in an age dominated by machinery. Employees were a commodity, easily replaced to perform monotonous tasks. Fortunately, things did not quite turn out like that. Although, for many, the workplace is still not ideal, today's machines are computers manipulated by us, rather than the other way around. The technology push in the first half of this century was mechanized automation, and the West became a world power based on its ability to manufacture and distribute goods. The technology push for the latter half of the century has been electronic information processing, enabling the West to become a world power based on its ability to synthesize and distribute information. So where is this expertise taking us? What will its impact be on the way corporations run and how we work in them? In order to understand the changing nature of the workplace let's have a brief look at the emergence of the information processing age.

A (Very) Short History of Computing

In the period between 1900 and 1940 factory mass production methods made enormous gains. While many different pieces of office equipment became available for arithmetic calculations and posting operations, most data processing operations still required a great deal of manual operation. World War II gave impetus to the development of improved data processing equipment for the office. There were three important reasons for this. First, there was a large increase in the amount of business data that had to be processed to manufacture the tremendous quantity of material needed for the war effort. To produce the thousands of warplanes required, an aircraft factory had to install intricate data processing systems for parts scheduling, ordering, inventory control and parts follow up. Often one plane contained parts made in over a thousand different manufacturing plants. Second, there was a big increase in business record keeping because of emergency government regulations, such as control over wages and raw materials. New taxes were imposed to pay for the war effort. Third, there was a shortage of labour available to do the increased data processing. When the war ended, many of the government demands on business, reports and statistics, and tax withholding continued. When business expanded to meet the growing need for consumer products, the requirement for data processing grew enormously. In the early 1950s, office jobs increased by 32 per cent while factory jobs increased by only 4 per cent. By 1960 the number of white collar workers in the USA finally outnumbered the factory workers. The rapid increase in office work created market pull for new techniques to process data more efficiently.

In 1954 General Electric used a large-scale scientific computer called UNIVAC to process payroll data. By 1960 over 50 models of computers were available for office use. By 1965 over 20,000 computers were being used in the USA for business data processing. These machines started a revolution which would change the nature of the enterprise forever – and for the better we hoped! During those early years computers were centralized machines, imprisoned in air conditioned humidified environments with raised flooring which hid miles of wires and cables.

The advent of the personal computer in the 1970s freed information processing from its sanitized prison. Popularized by a standard operating system MS-DOS, PCs gave us a common inexpensive platform which we have populated with a diversity of software which perhaps will eventually rival the diversity of life itself. Business applications migrated from centralized software on corporate mainframes to productivity tools running on PCs linked by servers. In the mid 1980s Sun Microsystems announced prophetically 'The Network is the Computer'. They were right. Within months early adopters of client server architectures used it as the corporate communications medium of choice. Electronic mail became the mandatory means of communication in high technology companies. A few small steps later and the Internet is *de facto* for any company needing to communicate in our information rich world. The advent of the World Wide Web gave us the easy to use desktop platform from which we can wander around the planet. (I wonder how many of you bought this book from amazon.com?)

So here we all are typing away in front of our PCs (me too as I write this). We're word processing, calculating, searching for facts, figures and information. We're checking the weather forecast for our fleets of ships, sending distress messages from sea, checking our competitors annual accounts and balance sheets, buying just about anything from a global shopping mall and even locating new friends, lovers and marriage partners. The reality is thankfully far removed from the *Metropolis* vision, but does it mean we are more efficient? Are we doing our jobs better? Maybe.

Data, Information and Knowledge

It is easy to be confused about the meaning of these three words. A lot of people incorrectly use them interchangeably.

Data are facts, pictures, numbers – presented without a context. Examples are Matson Crescent, green, 524-7812.

Information is organized data presented in context. Examples include organized statistics about houses in Australia, a schematic of a street, pictures organized in a medical book, an article in a journal.

Knowledge is information in context, together with an understanding of how to use it. Examples would include knowledge about drainage in a street, derived from looking at a schematic and understanding how the placement of houses may or may not affect drainage.

KM Concept#1

Knowledge = Information in Context + Understanding

In the business world, we need data, information and knowledge. Access comes in a myriad of ways; data, information and knowledge are derived from reading, talking to colleagues, noticing things in our environment. None is necessarily more important than the other. It all depends on the context of the scenario.

What is interesting is how the organization accesses and uses data, information and knowledge. The extent to which the organization can be said to be efficient is the extent to which it applies available data, information and knowledge to the problem at hand. Inefficient organizations reinvent processes, survey the same geographical area over and over again. The trick is making sure that access to knowledge, information and data is available to the right person, at the right time and in the right place. The process which seeks to satisfy this requirement is knowledge management. The employee who uses knowledge and wisdom in the place of work is a knowledge worker. It has been estimated by Betty Zucker at the Gottlieb School of Management in Zurich that as little as 20 per cent of the available and pertinent knowledge in a company is actually ever used. The knowledge management process seeks to improve on that figure, hopefully with positive consequences for the organization.

Data   🙁   Sequences of numbers, letters, pictures, etc. presented *without* a context

Information   🙂   Organized data, tables, sales statistics, a well presented talk when presented in context

Knowledge   🙂   Organized information together with understanding of what it means

Figure 1.1 Definitions

Knowledge is Underutilized in the Organization

THE KNOWLEDGE BASED ORGANIZATION

At this point it would be a mistake to conclude that anyone working in a high technology industry is a knowledge worker, and everyone else is not. What we need to discover is the extent to which the individual uses knowledge in his or her job, and then determine how critical his or her role is in the organization. There are all sorts of knowledge available in the organization, and many different ways of thinking about knowledge. The type of knowledge required by a company will determine the profile of the employee, the tools used and the training received. What is important for the manager in the organization is to have a deep understanding of these issues so that knowledge management processes can start to be put into place.

The number of companies reliant on knowledge has grown significantly over the last 50 years. Consider consulting companies. The product they sell is derived from the knowledge and wisdom of their consultants. The risk in consulting businesses is that employees with valuable expertise leave the company. In this case assets are directly linked to the individual.

Knowledge Adds Value

In some businesses knowledge provides real added value to the customer, for which they are prepared to pay a premium. Consider services offered by couriers such as Federal Express and DHL. Computerization has enabled these companies to provide a tracking system for customer packages. Now if I want to know the location of a package I can ask my local pickup point to tell me where it is and give me an estimated time of arrival. If a package gets lost – it can be tracked down by its computer coding, telling both the agent and the customer where it is most likely to be found. This is a value added service which provides knowledge to the customer about the delivery schedule of the package. In recent times it has become popular in the software industry to add value to ask design engineers to spend some time manning customer support desks. Putting the designer at the coal face with the customer might be a bit frightening for the engineer – but after dealing directly with customer complaints the added value to the engineering process is immeasurable and inexpensive. The alternative is to put the engineer at the end of a chain of Chinese whispers where the potency of the original message is usually diluted. I am reminded of an e-mail message called The Plan I first saw several years ago which arrived back in my e-mail recently – still continuing its missionary journey on the Internet:

KM Concept#3

Knowledge Adds Value to Products and Services

The Plan

In the beginning was The Plan, and then came the Assumptions, and the Assumptions were without form, and The Plan was completely without Substance, and Darkness was upon the faces of the workers.

And they spoke unto their group heads, saying: 'The Plan is a crock of s*** and it stinks.'

And the group heads went unto their managers and said unto them: 'It is a container of excrement and it is very strong, such that none here may abide it.'

And the managers went unto their director and said unto him: 'It is a vessel of fertiliser and none may abide its strength.'

And the director went unto the executive director and said: 'It contains that which promotes plant growth and it is very strong.'

And the executive director went unto the vice president and said unto him: 'It promotes growth and is very powerful.'

And the vice president went unto the president and said unto him: 'This powerful new Plan will actively promote the growth and efficiency of the department and this area in particular.'

And the president looked upon The Plan and saw that it was good, and The Plan became The Policy.

Knowledge Provides Competitive Edge

So what about the courier services that do not offer package tracking facilities? They may lose business due to the lack of a competitive advantage, or they have to respond in some fashion which demonstrates a superior service in some other way. Perhaps they take a leaf from the books of Continental Airlines and determine what their customers care about the most. For courier services it is likely to be the same as an airline service – on time. Given a choice between a tracking service and a guarantee to be on time most customers would choose the latter (actually it replaces the need for the former). Knowledge is a competitive advantage when it comes to providing all sorts of services to customers.

Would a Rose Smell as Sweet by any Other Name?

Customers like to buy products from people they think understand their problem and have knowledge of the type of solution they need. However having knowledge is not enough by itself, the company needs to be positioned in the mind of the prospect appropriately. This is what we call coupling of intangible assets. Just having the knowledge to, say, bring a product to market such as a computer, does not mean that people will buy the product from you if you don't have that position in their minds. This was clearly demonstrated by Xerox in the 1980s when they entered the computer market with their Star products, later their Artificial Intelligence workstations sold by a little known Xerox spinoff called En-Vos. Neither venture was successful, not because Xerox did not have a very fine computer product – they did – but because people do not buy computers from a company called Xerox. Xerox was positioned in the mind of the prospect as a copier company.

Knowledge of Facts Gets Lost

Think of employees who have worked for the company for many years. What do they know? Think of key people in marketing or sales, what do they know? Think of people you do not consider to be key players – what do they know? If you are certain they are not key players – would you be comfortable making them redundant tomorrow? Are you sure?

A few years ago a defence contractor won a contract to refurbish an aircraft, and the task required the removal of the wings from the plane. A pretty big problem – which became even bigger when they realized that all those employees who had that knowledge had left the company. At the same defence contractor during a small demonstration, a profile of the knowledge of one engineer picked at random was shown to a senior executive as a demonstration of how deep knowledge could be retrieved and captured. The executive remarked, 'I didn't know we had anyone working here with that level of expertise' – the employee had worked on every major European aeroplane to come to market over a 20 year period. The size of this organization is more than 20,000 employees – the majority of whom have worked for the company for more than 10 years. When you look at the corporate workforce as you know them, you are looking at the tip of an iceberg.

Knowledge is a Transient Asset

We know that knowledge is a transient asset. When employees leave the company they take all their knowledge with them. But when an employee just changes jobs within the same company over a very short period of time the new label which has been stuck on his or her forehead somehow gives the rest of us the impression that his or her memory has been erased at the same time. Not true. If the individual is a social animal he or she may migrate into the role of a 'gatekeeper', that is someone who knows how to find out things – we'll talk more about that later. In general it is very easy and very quickly done to forget exactly what people know. Asking everyone to write down what they know is not a practical alternative either – as they don't have time to document their own knowledge and work at the same time! And that is assuming it is possible to document the type of knowledge they possess. As an exercise try writing down how to ride a bicycle, in a manner appropriate for someone who has not seen one before.

Knowledge Based Industries

Knowledge based industries are those where the added value of the employees is the knowledge they possess, which typically can be transferred from one situation to another. Examples include:

1 all forms of engineering organizations;
2 all forms of research laboratories;
3 all forms of consulting houses;
4 all forms of marketing organizations;
5 all forms of sales organizations;
6 all forms of software organizations;
7 all forms of organizations that work on a 'project basis', such as lawyers;
8 all forms of recruiters and head hunters.

That's not to say that knowledge workers don't exist in manufacturing facilities – they do. In one study undertaken by The Technology Broker it was determined that only two individuals in the company really understood a particularly complex, and unpredictable manufacturing process. The company and its $15 million of revenue were at the mercy of just two individuals, neither of whom had ever documented their knowledge.

GLOBAL COMPETITION

One reason we have become so hungry to have knowledge in the right place at the right time is because our markets have become global, and understanding them is essential to success. For a huge number of businesses the world is split into three chunks: America, Asia Pacific and Europe, each representing about one third of the potential market. It's not difficult to see why so many companies become successful in America first, then move into the rest of the world. The USA is the largest homogeneous market in the world – but just being successful in Europe is not enough, so it's necessary to come to grips with Europe and Asia. Europe embodies 20 or more cultures, as does Asia Pacific. Customers outside the USA frequently like their products and services packaged to suit local tastes. They may also like them to be supported differently. Researching and responding to local market requirements requires capture of requirements, interpretation and the subsequent development of strategy. In addition regular monitoring of market movements is required. To the uninitiated this means buying and reading market research reports, to the seasoned marketing executive it means personal contact with opinion makers, customers and the competition. It means predicting what R&D competitors will be pursuing up to 5 years in advance. This type of knowledge and information can always be located, but it takes management of real market knowledge to use it to advantage. Market knowledge can exist in a variety of places in the organization – in the heads of the account executives and salesmen, in sales reports they may write. It may also exist in customer service reports and in the minds of service personnel who operate customer support telephone lines. It should also exist in the minds of marketing staff who undertake market analysis and talk to customers when preparing a marketing plan. Potentially useful knowledge is distributed throughout the company. It's frequently fragmented and the organization loses, as no one individual has access to the whole picture.

KM Concept#4

Knowledge Provides Competitive Advantage

Technology Push and Overload

The Internet has pushed us into overload. But it's information overload, and in many cases that information needs to be synthesized, put into context and then used as knowledge upon which corporate decisions can be made. There is a common misunderstanding that merely taking information from the Internet, databases and so forth, and organizing it into document form changes it into knowledge – it doesn't – what is missing is the interpretation of the relevance of the information in context to turn it into knowledge. Context is everything.

AGENTS AND USER PROFILING

One of the more interesting ways in which information can be delivered to us already 'in context' is if we have our own personal agents who know the types of things we are interested in, then they go and find them for us. It's like having your own personal detective who knows you are interested in Thai cuisine, or the life of Georgette Heyer, or aspects of knowledge management or even Formula 1 racing. Your personal 'intelligent agent' spends its life roaming the Internet looking for information it knows you are interested in. In order to do this, the agent needs to have a profile of the types of things its user is interested in. In some cases the software may ask the user to detail interests. In others (and sometimes both cases), software observes the search patterns of the individual and works out that they are interested in Formula 1. These 'intelligent agents' enable markets consisting of just one consumer to exist. This is a truly interesting notion for marketing executives to come to terms with. We love to segment markets. Divide and conquer. Find the special market niche for our products and services which means we know as much as possible about a homogeneous customer. When they are not homogeneous we don't like it. It means we have to customize the sales cycle for each individual. It takes longer to sell to a non-homogeneous market as customers are all different. You have to research each customer to take into account their personal preferences, and work out how best to sell to them. With single consumer markets all that changes. We now have the technology to customize products and services to the individual. One person – one market. So the trick for the marketing executive of the future is to know how to build products and services which can be tweaked to the exact needs and desires of the individual.

THE ASSETS OF THIRD MILLENNIUM COMPANIES

As we get nearer to the year 2000, it's only natural to think about the past and wonder about the future. Those of us who work in high technology companies have seen so many drastic changes in recent years and we wonder how we can measure success. Last night a colleague and I had to recommend a valuation for a client company wishing to raise venture capital finance. It's a software company with a revenue of $1.5 million, small profits, yet software and an amazing growth opportunity due to some legislation which will be introduced before the end of the millennium. If we look at the value of the software company what is there there? No physical assets, just some computers and other equipment, but you can buy a

PC for $1,000. No buildings or land. Actually the value in the company is derived from just four things:

1 the intellectual property rights which the company derives from ownership of the software;
2 knowledge of the market (in various employees' heads);
3 knowledge of how to build this particular type of software (in employees' heads);
4 the (as yet) unattained market share which is available to the company (the opportunity).

So in this case the value of the company has more to do with the availability of the opportunity to this particular company and its relative ability to grab that opportunity. If we looked at businesses in the first half of this century the valuation methods would have been very different to those used today. In 1940 the value would have been based on tangible assets. Today the value is increasingly based on intangible assets.

In their discussion paper on goodwill and intangible assets published in 1994, the UK Accounting Standards Board notes that in a survey of 370 acquisitions, it was found that the amount paid for purchased goodwill, as a percentage of acquirers' net worth, pre-acquisition, grew from 1 per cent in 1976 to 44 per cent in 1987. This fact supports the premise that there has been a substantial shift in the way companies are perceived as valuable. The market clearly believes there is more to a company than the tangible assets. The problem is that goodwill tends to be treated as a 'catch all', so even though it's possible to say that the intangible assets of the company have value, there usually isn't an itemized list. Some investors are extremely interested in exactly what constitutes the value of these intangible assets. Knowledge of the employees, the way the organization is (or isn't) managed is clearly an asset. Knowledge is linked to almost all functions in the company, so it's necessary to look at knowledge in the context of the way it is used inside the organization. This means looking at all of the intangible assets of a company, and that is what we call an intellectual capital audit.

2

Intellectual Capital – The Context for Knowledge Management

Intellectual capital is not new. It's been around since the first vendor established a good relationship with a customer. Then it was called good-will. What has happened over the last two decades is an explosion in key technical areas including information technology, the media and communications, giving us new tools with which we have built a global economy. Many of these tools bring intangible benefits, which never existed before and which we now take for granted. The organization can

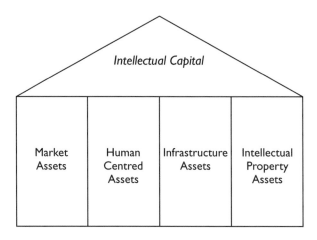

Figure 2.1 Corporate goals

no longer function without them, their ownership provides competitive advantage. Therefore they are an asset.

Intellectual capital is the term given to the combined intangible assets which enable the company to function.

THE COMPONENTS OF INTELLECTUAL CAPITAL

The intellectual capital of an enterprise can be split into four categories:

1 market assets;
2 intellectual property assets;
3 human centred assets;
4 infrastructure assets.

THE INTELLECTUAL CAPITAL METHOD

The intellectual capital method was developed by The Technology Broker[1] as a tool to assist in strategic planning and due diligence. Unlike other methods it only looks at intangible assets, which we hypothesize are more important to high growth, high technology companies than tangible assets. That's not to say that tangible assets such as buildings, machinery and plant are not important, but that they must be coupled to intangible assets in order for the company to grow and become valuable. Put simply, we are looking at the attributes of a company which do not appear on the balance sheet. The intellectual capital method (IC method) uses several indicators in order to evaluate a business opportunity: the goal, the intellectual capital, the dream ticket, the audit, the index, the target and the measures. Each of these indicators is described below.

The Goal

The goal is the reason the assets are being measured. For example a company may want to have a 10 per cent growth in market share. The IC method would identify the assets required to achieve the goal and determine their relative strength or weakness. Thus the goal provides the context for the audit. It is not possible to measure the assets in the absence of a goal, as their relative strength or weakness is goal dependent. So assets which were weak to support a 10 per cent growth in market share, could be strong to support 5 per cent growth.

The Intellectual Capital

Intellectual capital is split into four categories, market assets, intellectual property assets, infrastructure assets and human centred assets. Each of these categories is described below.

Market Assets

Market assets are those which belong to the company and give it power in the marketplace. They include brands, positioning, customer base, company name, backlog, distribution channels, collaborations, franchise agreements, licensing agreements, favourable contracts and so on.

Why are Market Assets Important?

Market assets are important because they give a company a competitive advantage in the marketplace. Branding denotes ownership and identity of products and services; customer loyalty ensures repeat sales leading to a healthy backlog. A good distribution channel ensures the entire market of potential customers can be serviced and that revenues from product and service sales is maximized. Favourable contracts ensure less expensive or guaranteed service, such as advertising or product sales, giving a company an advantage over its competitors who may not enjoy similar privileges. Market assets ensure that customers know the identity of the company and what it does. From time to time a company mismanages its marketing strategy and generates confusion in the marketplace. When customers are confused they don't buy. Effective positioning strategies ensure that when a customer hears a company name the thought that enters the mind of the customer is the thought the company would wish him or her to have. Huge sums of money are put behind promotional campaigns which reinforce positioning strategies. 'At Avis we try harder', 'Beans Means Heinz', 'Intel Inside' and so on.

┌─ KM Concept#5 ───────────────────────────────────

Knowledge of Markets is a Business Weapon

└──

Table 2.1 Audit methods for market centred assets

	Customer survey	Customer interview	Analyse sales	Analyse cost of sale	Market research	Audit agreements	Competitive analysis	Determine ROI	Analyse payments
Service brands	✔	✔			✔		✔	✔	
Product brands	✔	✔			✔		✔	✔	
Corporate brands	✔	✔			✔		✔	✔	
Champions		✔			✔				
Customers		✔			✔				
Evangelists		✔			✔				
Customer loyalty	✔	✔			✔		✔	✔	
Repeat business	✔	✔	✔	✔	✔		✔	✔	
Company name	✔	✔			✔			✔	
Backlog			✔		✔		✔	✔	✔
Distribution channels	✔	✔	✔	✔	✔	✔	✔	✔	✔
Business collaborations		✔	✔	✔	✔	✔	✔	✔	✔
Franchise agreements			✔	✔	✔	✔	✔	✔	✔
Licensing agreements			✔	✔	✔	✔	✔	✔	✔
Favourable contracts	✔	✔	✔	✔	✔	✔	✔	✔	

Intellectual Property Assets

Intellectual property assets are properties of the mind and belong to the company. They are protectable in law. These assets include patents, copyright, design rights, trade secrets, trade marks and so on.

Why is Intellectual Property Important?

Intellectual property represents the legal mechanism for protecting many corporate assets. New devices leading to products or their component parts can be protected by one or more patents. Patents are valuable as they give the owner a monopoly on the patented invention for a period of time which is typically from 17–20 years; it varies from country to country. Patents are of particular value when they are embedded in products as the patent protects them from others who may want to copy the invention. Copyright protects the written word and is typically used to protect books, music and computer software. Market assets such as brands are protected by trade and service marks. Finally, trade secrets are protected by non-disclosure agreements, which means that the party who becomes privy to the secret agrees not to tell anyone other than those identified in the non-disclosure agreement. That said, the best way to keep a trade secret is not to tell anybody. The highest profile trade secret is probably the Coca-Cola formula, which is reputed to be shared between two individuals, each knowing half the formula!

Table 2.2 Audit methods for intellectual property assets

	Survey for market pull	Competitor analysis	Determine ROI	Audit agreements	ROI legal fees	Survey know-how	Analyse payments	Identify know-how
Patent	✔	✔	✔	✔	✔	✔	✔	✔
Copyright	✔	✔	✔	✔	✔	✔	✔	✔
Design rights	✔	✔	✔	✔	✔	✔	✔	✔
Semiconductor topography rights	✔	✔	✔	✔	✔	✔	✔	✔
Trade secrets	✔	✔	✔	✔	✔	✔	✔	✔
Trade marks	✔	✔	✔	✔	✔	✔	✔	✔
Service marks	✔	✔	✔	✔	✔	✔	✔	✔

┌─ KM Concept#6 ──┐
│   │
│   Knowledge is the Basis for Creating Intellectual Property │
│   │
└──┘

Infrastructure Assets

Infrastructure assets are a wide range of assets which include management philosophy, corporate culture, management and business processes, financial relations, methodologies and IT systems which enable the organization to function. Examples include methodologies for assessing risk, methods of managing a sales force, financial structure, databases of information on the market or customers, communication systems such as e-mail and teleconferencing systems. Basically, infrastructure assets are the elements which make up the way the organization works. These assets belong to the company. But we are not talking about the value of the tangibles which comprise the computer system and so on, but the impact of its use in the organization. A good example is the Internet. Use of the Internet is free. It also doesn't belong to anyone, so it won't appear on anyone's balance sheet. However, the ability to use the Internet to sell goods means it is providing the organization with a distribution channel, therefore it is an asset. Such assets are peculiar to each business and their value to the organization can only be attained by survey. Sadly, the acquisition of infrastructure assets is frequently the result of some crisis, positioning them as a necessary evil rather than as the structure which makes the organization strong and efficient.

Why are Infrastructure Assets Important?

Infrastructure assets are important because they bring order, safety, correctness and quality to the organization. They also provide a context for the employees of the organization to work and communicate with each other.

Marketing the value of infrastructure assets to the individual within the organization is important, in order to ensure that all individuals understand what they are supposed to do in given situations and how they contribute to the achievement of corporate goals. However, infrastructure assets should not be perceived as law and must change and bend to reflect changes in the market and workplace. Organizations which do not regularly question the value and effectiveness of infrastructure assets lose the edge which makes them win in the marketplace.

Human Centred Assets

Human centred assets comprise the collective expertise, creative and problem solving capability, leadership, entrepreneurial and managerial skills embodied by the employees of the organization. They also include psychometric data and indicators on how individuals may perform in given situations, such as in a team or under stress. We promote a viewpoint that we are not only looking at an individual in order to perform a particular job function, but view the individual as a dynamic entity who may fit into a variety of jobs over time. It is the job of a good manager to ensure that each human 'asset' has access and opportunity to mechanisms which enable the employee to achieve his or her full potential within the organization.

Why are Human Centred Assets Important?

Human centred assets are the qualities which make up people. It may seem silly to ask why people are important but it's worth thinking about for a while. There are no businesses which can operate without at least one person. However, unlike market, intellectual and infrastructure assets, human centred assets cannot be owned by the company. This should mean that they receive special treatment, but sadly they often do not.

Humans are expensive to hire, train and sustain. They also have the right to leave their employment, get sick, go on holiday and in general

Table 2.3 Audit methods for infrastructure assets

	Survey state-of-art	Determine ROI	Determine fit for purpose	Determine added value	Interview customers	Interview employees	Assess standards
Management philosophy	✔		✔	✔	✔	✔	✔
Corporate culture	✔	✔	✔	✔	✔	✔	✔
Management processes	✔	✔	✔	✔	✔	✔	✔
Information technology systems	✔	✔	✔	✔	✔	✔	✔
Financial relations	✔	✔	✔	✔	✔	✔	
Required standards	✔	✔	✔	✔	✔		✔

damage themselves via a wide range of hobbies and pastimes. As they become proficient and then excel in their employment, they learn more and become more valuable. But the knowledge in the head of the individual belongs to the person – not the company. So it's important to understand the skills, knowledge and expertise of the individual in order to know how and why someone is valuable and what role he or she should play within the organization. The optimal position for the organization to be in is to be able to derive maximum benefit from an individual being in employment with the company. That should be balanced by way of compensation – monetary, professional, personal development and opportunity. To do this properly is time consuming. Don't just consider the cost – but whether or not the third millennium enterprise can afford not to do it.

> ┌─ KM Concept#7 ─────────────────────────────
>
> ## Knowledge, Like People, is Transient

The Dream Ticket

The dream ticket describes the set of assets which have to be present in order for the goal to be met. It describes an idealized state, which describes the optimal position the company could be in to achieve the goal. For example two elements of a dream ticket to improve sales could be:

Table 2.4 Audit methods for human centred assets

	Interview	Test and assess	Knowledge elicitation	Self-assessment	Manager assessment	Peer review	Assessment record
Education	✔						✔
Vocational qualifications	✔	✔		✔	✔	✔	
Work related knowledge	✔		✔	✔	✔	✔	✔
Occupational potential	✔	✔					
Personality	✔	✔					
Work related competencies	✔		✔	✔	✔	✔	✔

1 That all customers who had ever bought from us will buy again within six months.
2 That all potential customers recognize our brand name.

Identification of the elements of the dream ticket makes it possible to couple, rank and prioritize them. Some will be more important than others. Some may be pointless to pursue until others are in place.

The Audit

The audit is the activity of gathering information on the relative strength or weakness of the elements of the dream ticket. There are over 30 audit methods used depending upon which asset is being measured. For example if you wanted to measure brand recognition, a survey would need to be completed. If it was know-how of a certain, identified topic it would be ascertained by knowledge elicitation. If the value of some form of infrastructure needed to be determined, fit-for-purpose may be an issue. Like the assets, audit methods are selected depending upon the context.

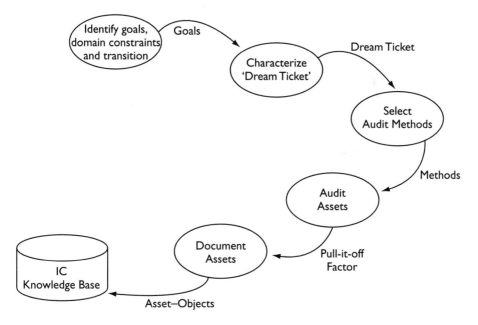

Figure 2.2 Intellectual capital audit process

The Index

The index is constructed following an audit of the asset and a comparison of its status with that of the dream ticket. If the status of the asset matches the dream ticket it is ranked at 5, if it is very weak, it is ranked at 1, and if the company did not even know the asset was required it is ranked at zero.

The Target

The target shows the status of all assets in one representation. It is split into four quadrants reflecting each asset category. The size of the quadrant is not related to its importance. A directional arrow shows whether the asset is becoming stronger (and moving toward the centre of the target), or weaker (moving away). The target provides us with a snap-shot of the company with respect to its strengths, weaknesses and whether the situa-

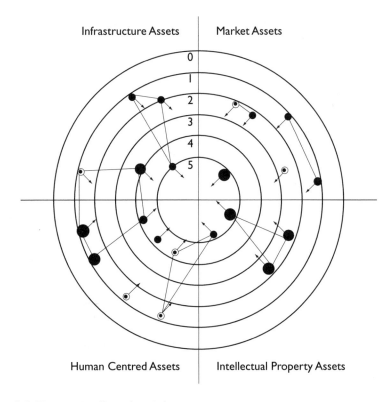

Figure 2.3 Targeting intellectual capital

tion is expected to become better or worse. In addition, coupling between assets is shown, as implementing measures to improve a situation could be attempts to fix symptoms rather than illnesses.

The Measures

The measures are those actions which can be implemented in order to improve the status of assets over time. Some measures will have impact quickly, such as the impact of a television advertisement campaign on name recognition. Others by their nature will take a period of time before they have impact on the asset. Examples include the impact of training programmes on the know-how of engineers who design silicon chips. Assets will need to be audited again over a period of time to determine whether they have become stronger or weaker. Thus the measures are evaluated. A second audit shows how assets have moved on the target. This enables us to use the intellectual capital method as a management tool.

Why is Intellectual Capital Important?

One hundred years ago labour was cheap. The value of the enterprise was measured in terms of smokestacks, machinery and cash. In the third millennium labour will not be cheap. The human centred assets a company needs to operate will be rare and expensive commodities. It will take years of investment to create valuable market, infrastructure and intellectual property assets. Many companies, especially service oriented businesses, don't need many tangible assets to exist. Computers, communications and knowledge provide corporate bedrock for third millennium companies.

The market is homogenizing. No single organization brought about the change. It resulted from the widespread use of communications, information technology and the use of the media. The market has expanded for most growing businesses and at the same time has become more accessible. A trade mark which was only meaningful in a local community at the beginning of the century can now be known all over the globe. Twenty years ago we were not interested in intellectual capital. Its emerging importance reflects the organization's increasing dependence on intangible assets. New types of companies are born every day which have only intangible assets. Their products are intangible and can be distributed electronically in the 'market space' via the Internet. Such media and knowledge intensive companies whose products are digital are third millennium enterprises. The world has changed again and we must find new ways of monitoring and managing the organization which reflect that change.

THE INTELLECTUAL CAPITAL INDICATOR

Answer true or false to the following statements:

1 In my company every employee knows what his or her job is and how it contributes to corporate goals.
2 In my company each employee is treated as a rare asset, and management strive to fit each person into the optimal job.
3 Every employee in my company has the opportunity to create a career plan with the company.
4 In my company we evaluate ROI on R&D.
5 In my company we identify know-how generated by R&D.
6 In my company we know who our repeat customers are.
7 In my company we evaluate ROI on the distribution channel.
8 In my company we have a proactive intellectual property strategy.
9 In my company we audit all our licensing deals.
10 In my company we ensure there is synergy between employee learning programmes and corporate goals.
11 In my company the position we have in the mind of the prospect is the same as we promote.
12 In my company we know the value of our brands.
13 In my company every scientist and engineer understands the rudiments of patent protection.
14 In my company we generate new intellectual capital through business collaboration.
15 In my company our management processes make us strong.
16 In my company there is the infrastructure to help the employees do a good job.
17 In my company there is a mechanism to capture employees' recommendations to improve any aspect of the business.

18 In my company employees are quickly rewarded for helping the company to achieve its corporate goals.

19 In my company we understand the innovation process and encourage all employees to participate within it.

20 In my company our corporate culture is one of our greatest strengths.

The more 'false' answers you have given the more you need to focus on strengthening your company's intellectual capital.

Notes

[1] *Intellectual Capital: Core Asset for the Third Millenium Enterprise* by Annie Brooking published by International Thomson Business Press, 1996.

3

Dream On – Knowing What You Need to Know

In order to manage knowledge within the organization some decisions have to be made. What knowledge is important? Where do we start? Should we manage the knowledge of all employees or just a select few. Which select few? Should we get everyone to document what they know? Wait a minute . . . if they are documenting everything they know when do they have time to do their jobs? It's a conundrum, let's not even get into whether or not it's possible to document all the types of knowledge a company must be interested in.

The solution is as usual to focus; to look at the types of knowledge which are essential to the company in order to enable it to achieve its corporate goals. We've looked at intellectual capital in the context of corporate goals, and in some way knowledge is threaded through all aspects of the company, infrastructure, market assets and intellectual property. So to determine which knowledge is the most important, the best thing to do is to create a dream ticket, or a hierarchy of dream tickets.

DREAM TICKET

As we discussed in the previous chapter, a dream ticket is a set of critical assets which have to be in place in order to have a home run with a corporate goal. It may be the case that the goal can be achieved with a sub-optimal set of assets – but the dream ticket outlines the perfect world, the absolute perfect set of assets which could probably never be put in place. The ticket is comprised of four categories – each reflecting a quadrant of intellectual capital, market assets, intellectual property assets, infrastructure assets and human centred assets. Take the example of a company that wanted to generate $1 million in licence revenues from four biotechnology patents, A, B, C and D. The sub-set of assets that would ensure that the business would be successful might look as outlined below.

Market Assets

1 All companies that manufacture drugs will license patents A and D.
2 All companies that wish to prolong the life of their drugs license patent B.
3 Branding for the four patents is granted and global.
4 Brand recognition for the four patents is in excess of 70 per cent of the customer base.
5 That a marketing campaign is put in place to close 30 per cent of the market within 12 months.

All of the above are assets which give the company power in the marketplace. Numbers 4 and 5 imply that a competent person exists to put the marketing plan in place. So that competence needs to be reflected in the human centred assets listed further below.

Infrastructure Assets

6 There is a royalty auditing system to ensure payments are made.
7 That a system is put in place to locate companies which may be breaching the patent.

Both of the above assets are systems which will need someone to design them and the experience to implement them.

Intellectual Property Assets

8 That patents are granted for all four assets.
9 That new patents to strengthen the portfolio are generated within months.
10 That violation of the patents is easy to detect.

There is an obvious link between intellectual property and human centred assets. New intellectual property is generated by smart people with the appropriate wisdom to create new innovative products and processes.

Human Centred Assets

11 That key employees have the wisdom to create new intellectual property.
12 That key employees know how to put licensing deals together.
13 That key employees understand intellectual property law.
14 That key employees can design and manage systems to protect and exploit intellectual property.
15 That key employees understand the biopharmaceutical industry.

The set of human centred assets above are essential with respect to the goals of this particular company.

The assets outlined above all represent knowledge and wisdom which would enable the biotechnology company to achieve their corporate goal: to achieve $1 million in licence revenues. The next step would be to measure the relative strength of each of the elements on the dream ticket. This activity forms the main body of an intellectual capital audit, the process which looks at the strengths and weaknesses of the company as if taking a snap-shot. Where the assets are strong the company is in good shape to achieve its corporate goal. Where the assets are weak, measures have to be put in place to strengthen the assets.

┌─ KM Concept#8 ─────────────────────────────

   Dream Tickets Give Us Knowledge to Achieve Goals

CRITICAL KNOWLEDGE FUNCTIONS

Where human centred assets show up on a dream ticket they indicate that particular knowledge or competencies are necessary for the goal in question to be achieved. In this context they are critical knowledge functions in the company. This could be a particularly dangerous situation for a company to slide into, as the demise of the employees in possession of rare knowledge can have a devastating effect on the company. Where critical knowledge functions are missing from the organization it indicates that the company does not have the right profile of staff it requires to achieve its corporate goal. This would then indicate that the company needed to determine whether critical knowledge could be grown organically within the organization, or needs to be acquired by recruiting new employees from outside the organization.

Types of Critical Knowledge

There are various types of knowledge which can be critical in a company. Some examples might include:

1 Knowledge of a particular job such as how to remove the wings from an aircraft or how to clean out a boiler.
2 Knowledge of who knows what in a company.
3 Knowledge of how to get things done in a company – using the culture to maximum effect.
4 Knowledge of who is best to perform a particular job or task.
5 Knowledge of corporate history, why the company works the way it does.

6 Knowledge of a particular customer account.

7 Knowledge of a geography, country and its business customs.

8 Knowledge of how to put together a team that can achieve a particular task.

9 Knowledge of how to approach a particular problem which is difficult to solve.

The interesting thing about critical knowledge is that what is critical or otherwise changes depending upon the business context. The trick is also knowing who is in possession of what type of knowledge. What is critical today may not be critical tomorrow. The magic word is context. The relative value of knowledge changes depending upon what is happening in the company at any point in time. Let's take a look at the nature of some of these critical knowledge functions.

1 Knowledge of a Particular Job

Knowledge of a specific job can be as trivial as how to raise an invoice or how to design a nuclear reactor experiment. Not knowing how to raise an invoice when your assistant is on holiday and you need to buy something urgently can become hugely expensive and time consuming, especially if no one else is around who can make the problem go away. Sometimes knowledge of a particular function is very rare, and very valuable. We were asked to work with a scientist in Italy called Alan whose job was to design experiments which would predict the way in which the wall of a nuclear reactor would behave under certain explosion conditions. To perform this task Alan used a huge piece of software called Simmer. Simmer had been built to simulate the behaviour of the reactor, and was a really old piece of computer code which had never been documented properly. Alan had been designing experiments that used Simmer for nearly two decades. He was an expert in using the code. His expertise had been built on lots of experiential work. He 'knew' how the code would behave under certain conditions but was not aware of how the code itself worked as the rationale for its functioning had never been written down. Alan was the last of his generation to use the code. Experiments he designed took weeks to set up, then, on the appointed day he would modify a huge batch of punched cards, submit it to the computer and wait until the next day for the results of the experiment. The following day the computer would spit out a six-inch computer printout, which was unintelligible to anyone – except Alan, who would immediately skip to say page 184, look at column 43 across the top, on line 17 and either smile or come out with an expletive! Success or failure indicated in a heartbeat.

Three months later, after talking with Alan almost every day, we began to get a notion of how he designed his experiments, and how he interpreted the results of the computer run. Sadly the code itself was so badly written it was decided that a new way had to be determined to run the experiments. When Alan retires his knowledge will be lost forever.

KM Concept#9

Identify Critical Knowledge Functions

Don't Get Run over by a Truck

In America people ask of key employees – 'What would happen if he got run over by a truck?'. Mostly the question is not taken seriously – but it is not as silly as it sounds.

Recently we performed an intellectual capital audit at a company which made an unusual type of fibre. The company had never achieved its expected growth. One reason for this was that the quality of the end product was difficult to predict as the process itself was quite unpredictable. The plant and process had been designed some years earlier by a scientist who was no longer with the company, and the loss of expertise took several years to recover. Surprised that the company would be careless enough to lose such a key individual we asked why he had left. 'Oh he was run over by a taxi,' replied the CEO. 'He was the only one who really understood the process, and it took years for us to figure out how it worked as it had never been documented. Even now, although we understand a lot more than we did, and our quality has improved significantly there are still a lot of questions we can't answer.'

2 Knowledge of Who Knows What in a Company

Is there someone in your company who seems to spend most of their time talking to people, having coffee and, believe it or not, reading? What do they do? They don't appear to have any line responsibility, get invited to meetings yet never seem to take any action items? Who are they? Well there are two alternatives. The first would suggest that they are wasters, people who seem to know how to manipulate the organization to their own advantage, and do nothing – so perhaps someone should fire them. There is however an alternative. Maybe this person is a gatekeeper. Someone who knows who can answer questions and solve problems. They know answers to all sorts of questions because they 'read an article in a journal last week' or 'attended a workshop on that last year'. They spend their time networking, circulating, talking to everybody. Quite frequently they are people who have worked in the organization for many, many years. They are the human organizational historian and memory. The problem is recognizing them for what they are – a waster or a gatekeeper. If you fire a gatekeeper you sever links to the past. Like blasting a hole in the middle of a spider's web which has taken many years to construct. This is a huge mistake and it is very difficult to fix it.

--- KM Concept#10 ---

Know Who Knows What in the Company

3 Knowledge of How to Get Things Done in a Company – Using the Culture to Maximum Effect

Knowing how to get things done in a company can be very difficult as it means not only knowing about corporate procedures, but about the do's and don'ts of behaviour within that culture. Different cultures have different values, rituals and taboos. New employees have to confront this situation all the time, until they understand for themselves how 'things get done around here'. This may seem like a transient type of knowledge as once you know, you know. Not so. In our dynamic organization the rules can change from time to time, and of course as managers come and go the rules may also change. The people in the organization who seem to master this type of knowledge very well are the administrators and caretakers. The invisible network of secretaries and administrators in an organization is indeed formidable.

This type of knowledge takes on an interesting perspective when the knowledgeable person is an outsider to the organization. Consider an account manager who has been selling to a large corporation for a long time. Their account management skills will include the way in which that corporation works, and to his own organization that is a very valuable asset.

4 Knowledge of Who is Best to Perform a Particular Job or Task

Choosing the right person for the right job requires knowledge about both the individual and the job at hand. Perhaps the issue is career development. Perhaps it's the right mix between problem and individual or client and individual. Not many of us will refer to the psychometric profile of an individual before we assign a person to a job. Some managers 'just know'. Some have no idea how to use the talents of employees who work for the organization, and use their power to punish and inhibit the progress of the individual. A colleague of ours working for a government department in the UK was told by his boss that he would never be given an overseas post for which he was superbly qualified because as he said 'I just don't like you'.

5 Knowledge of Corporate History, Why the Company Works the Way it Does

Knowing about corporate history, how and why the company grew to be the organization it is today can also be really important knowledge to preserve. It provides the context for current and future activities. It is also valuable to ensure that work, including mistakes are not repeated.

6 Knowledge of a Particular Customer Account

We have a client we have been trying to do business with for four years. Three times we have agreed the start of a project, had the resources assigned and then it has been cancelled at the last minute. Once we agreed to do some 'preparatory work' for the client by way of looking at a market for some computer technology they had – having proved the market existed we were then put on hold to start the project, for months. Some time later we hired a new business development manager who also pursued the account, and once again was asked if we would do a little something in return for yet another project. Quite by accident the business development manager was overheard talking about the account and someone said – 'If you look in the archives you will find three huge files on this company. The amount of free work we have done in good faith over the years is substantial. Why not take the files to the client – dump them on his desk and say – this is how much work we have done for you over the last few years in an attempt to build a relationship with you and you have never paid us a penny. So NO this time if you want us to work for you sign on the dotted line, and we want to be paid in advance.'

The business development manager acted out his part. He got the deal signed, and we got paid an advance payment. Then guess what happened? Exactly, they 'put the project on hold'. A lack of serendipity can be expensive. Organizations just can't afford to have valuable intelligence on the market and customers drop into their lap by chance. This type of knowledge is not only valuable it can also be a competitive advantage, and as such needs to be managed.

┌─ KM Concept#11 ───┐
│   │
│   Knowledge About Customers Makes Selling Easier   │
│   │
└──┘

7 Knowledge of a Geography, Country and its Business Customs

Knowledge of how to behave in a business context can mean the difference between winning an account and losing it. For many of us mastering the art of doing business in another culture is harder than starting the company, inventing the product and bringing it to market. Employees who understand the nuances of doing business with other cultures have knowledge which is difficult to transfer from one person to another; you just have to have had the experience. Sometimes this is memorable, as a friend recounted to me several years ago.

On a business trip to Japan an American colleague joined a group of businessmen for dinner. He was a conservative diner at the best of times and was quite terrified of what he might be asked to eat in Japan. Nevertheless in true Silicon Valley style he determined to do whatever it took to win the business and joined in a joint dinner enthusiastically. At one point during the meal each person was presented with a small bowl with a variety of content. However the content of his bowl was still wriggling about. A small live squid was on the menu. He frantically looked about the table to see his Japanese colleagues pick it up with their chopsticks, and it cartwheel gracefully into their mouths. After a gulp of saki he determined to followed suit, grabbed the squid and shoved it into his mouth. Unfortunately graceful cartwheels did not occur as the squid fought like stink to get out of his mouth. Little legs popped out here and there, which he quickly shoved back in before anyone would notice. Alas, too late, as by now he was the centre of attention, his hosts looking at him in horror as he resolved to firmly bite the squid to death and swallow hard. Later, but not later enough for him, he was politely informed that it was barbaric to eat live things at the dinner table and it was the custom to kill the animal by stabbing it through the brain with his chopsticks. He did win the business!

8 Knowledge of How to Put Together a Team that can Achieve a Particular Task

Knowledge of how to put together teams can be a critical knowledge function where teamwork is essential for the operation of the organization. In some organizations where teamwork is mission critical the strength of the team can literally mean the difference between life and death. In such cases it might not be possible for managers to personally know each of the people in the team, and great reliance might be put on a variety of psychometric tests, dry running an operation in a simulated environment many times. The expertise to set up, monitor and measure such scenarios is valuable to organizations that need to be certain in advance how team members will behave under a variety of circumstances.

> ┌─ KM Concept#12 ─────────────────────
> │
> │   Knowledge About People Means Better Teams
> │

9 Knowledge of How to Approach a Particular Problem which is Difficult to Solve

Some people know how to think about problems. This type of knowledge frequently comes with experience and a kind of confidence that eventually you 'will' know how to solve something you don't currently understand how to do. Linked to psychometric abilities which can be measured, such as analytical skills, this type of knowledge is valuable, especially when it is exhibited by leaders. Such individuals possess a sort of self-awareness accompanied by spiritual strength. They just seem to know that they have the knowledge to solve a problem even though they can't access it right now.

Critical Knowledge Can be Transient

It's important not to fall into a false sense of security when considering critical knowledge in the organization, as it may be the case that know-how which is important today, this month or this year is not important next year. Understanding the dynamics of the business is important in manipulating the organization to perform as best it can every day. So developing dream tickets is an ongoing process in the light of the goals of the organization, department or even the team. The dream ticket method works at a variety of levels of granularity, so in an organizational setting there could be a hierarchy of dream tickets whose elements will change as the organization moves through time. If it's important this quarter to put an infrastructure in place to monitor royalty payments, and that goal is achieved then another will no doubt replace it, such as an element reflecting the quality of the audit and so forth.

MANAGING MERGERS AND ACQUISITIONS

Consider the situation where a company decides to acquire another company. Managing the successful integration of a company is a real art. The companies need to come together without killing each other, losing key employees or losing access to valuable corporate knowledge. This is a difficult time for the company which is being acquired and many employees are nervous, wondering whether or not they will be made redundant, get a boss they don't like and so forth. In this situation, executives who can manage the seamless integration of two companies are extremely valuable. But what do you do with them once the integration is complete? If they are very successful they are not needed. Yet the expertise is enormously valuable in the context of merging two companies – once they are merged it's not valuable at all. Mostly such individuals move on after a successful merger, next time the expertise has to be relearnt by someone new and valuable time is wasted again and again.

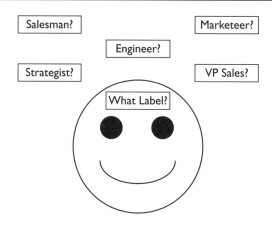

Figure 3.1 Labelled for lost knowledge

LABELLED FOR LOST KNOWLEDGE?

In most companies individual employees have job titles which in some way reflect the job they are currently paid to perform. This can be a huge disadvantage when it comes to tapping into the corporate knowledge base. Take an individual, Harry, who has worked for a company for 25 years as a design engineer. He is currently working on the design of a cockpit for a new aeroplane, Plane A, when a job to refurbish an old plane, Plane B, is won by his company. The team that has been assigned to work on Plane B has lots of problems to solve, many of which concern refurbishment of the cockpit. The B Team have never worked with Harry, and he is working in a different office on the other side of the country. Harry has the knowledge and capability to shave 20 per cent of the time spent on the cockpit refurbishment as he assisted in the design of the cockpit of Plane B some years before. However, at that time he was just a junior, and his boss was the one who was known to be the expert on the cockpit of Plane B. How can the organization remember that Harry can advise Team B? Maybe Harry should even be leading Team B? In reality Team B will probably have to spend weeks rediscovering knowledge that Harry already has. This is primarily because Harry's job and job title are currently related to Plane A. Links to his past are severed by his job title, and his past is not available to Team B. This situation is in fact commonplace in almost every type of company, no matter how small. In giving our employees labels and titles we actually mismanage the perception of their capabilities.

What's in a Name?

In an economy where things move fast and situations change dynamically, organizations that wish to succeed must also mirror that behaviour. Business situations can change overnight, and the response by the organizations must also be overnight. This implies that organizations must be much more flexible than they have been in the past, teams coming together and dissembling as the situation requires. Consulting companies have worked in this way for many years. This month Jack is the boss and Harry and Sue work for him. Next month Sue is the boss and Jack her subordinate. This has less to do with titles and more to do with context. If the business requires that solution, that's the right approach. The basis for retaining employment is to be a valuable player in the corporate game of survival, and this has less to do with titles, and more to do with capabilities. Capable employees are valuable, and as such should be paid more. So the name of the top job is the most capable in the context of the need of the business day.

KM Concept#13

Job Titles Mask Knowledge About People

Job Titles Position People

Positioning is managing perception in the mind of the prospect. Positioning a person within the organization is done by way of their job title. Ask yourself what you would expect of people with the following job titles:

1 Director of Sales;
2 Director of Marketing;
3 Director of Sales and Marketing.

Which of the above three is most likely to fail at their job – and why?

I once met a man on a plane whose job title was Corporate Jester. I asked him what he did. He said his job was to question corporate policy, the decisions of key executives and almost anything in general that was going on in the company. His job was to ask the questions that no one else had the courage to ask. Wow – what a great job! Of course the requirement

Figure 3.2 Who's your corporate jester?

for the job is far removed from being a fool – quite the opposite, as was the requirement for being Court Jester centuries ago.

COMPETENCIES, PROFICIENCIES, CAPABILITIES AND CRITICAL KNOWLEDGE FUNCTIONS

Having a lot of smart people working in a company does not mean that the company is probably going to succeed. The way in which the competencies and capabilities of the company are utilized and grown will have an impact on the extent to which the organization is successful. The terms competencies, core competencies, capabilities and critical knowledge functions are frequently confused. Different people have different definitions. Here I present my definitions, together with a rationale for how everything fits together.

A competence is an ability typically gained as a result of learning or training such as attending a course. A doctor who has recently qualified has a certificate which states that he or she is competent to perform the job of doctor. After several years, that competence is enhanced by knowledge gained from 'doing' the job. New competencies will have been learned either from reading medical journals, attending training courses or indeed by observation, abstraction and so forth. The more the doctor practises his or her craft the more proficient he or she will become. So proficiency tends to track competency. Examples of a competence would be to design an undercarriage, make a gateau, write computer code and so forth. However some people are more competent than others at designing undercarriage, making gateaux, and writing computer code. So it's useful to understand the extent to which an individual is both proficient and competent. Figure 3.3, developed by Karl Wiig, is an excellent way of demonstrating how the two are related. The basic principle is clear – learn first, then keep doing it until you get better, then learn something else, and so on. By following the cycle an individual grows from being an innocent to a grand master.

One of the reasons I like Karl's model so much is that you can apply your own definitions within your particular company and everybody understands the general concept without needing to know the detail. Karl's definitions for each of the levels of proficiency are as follows:

Ignorant — Totally unaware, with no understanding or judgement

Beginner — Vaguely aware of the field – innocent with no real experience

Advanced beginner — Aware and partially informed but relatively unskilled

Competent performer — Beginning deeper understanding – narrowly skilled

Proficient performer — Competent and broadly skilled – knowledgeable in selected areas

Expert — Highly proficient in a particular area – generally knowledgeable

Master — Highly expert in many areas and broadly knowledgeable

Grand master — World class expert in all areas of the knowledge domain.

So if a CEO says, 'We are an engineering company where 50 per cent of our staff are proficient grand masters in Formula 1 chassis design' – that means something to me, even though I don't understand the detail of the job of chassis design. Alternatively he could say '50 per cent of our staff are

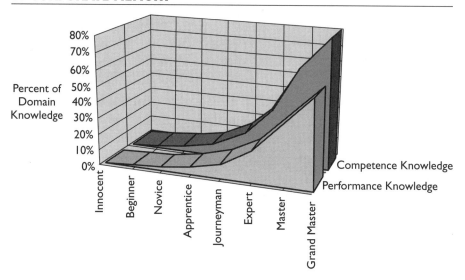

Figure 3.3 A hypothetical model for how competence and performance knowledge may grow with increasing proficiency

Ph.D. qualified'. What does that mean to me? – just that lots of smart people work at the company.

The model is very flexible and each company can take the scale, innocent to grand master, and determine exactly what job specific competencies and proficiencies would represent which point on the scale. The model works for environmental engineers, programmers, whatever – because each company can determine what each level means. In the UK there is an initiative called NVQ, which links nicely into this model. The NVQ system was established as employers did not know what qualifications from different colleges and universities actually meant in terms of competence. NVQ is a national system with a definition so NVQ levels are applied to a huge variety of competencies.

┌─ KM Concept#14 ─────────────────────────────

Proficient People are Competent and have Experience

If we return to the concept of dream ticket in order to perform a job, say refurbish the cockpit of a plane, there will be several competencies required from various individuals who are proficient to perform the task. The combination of desired competence and proficiency means that the organization has a capability to perform a task – such as refurbish a cockpit. If all of the competencies are present, but the individuals are not proficient, the organization does not have the capability.

When determining critical knowledge functions these will include the set of capabilities without which the job cannot be done. They may also be critical because the expertise is rare, difficult to move from one person to another – yet without it the task at hand cannot be performed.

If a company made its living from designing cockpits there would be a set of critical knowledge functions for Plane A, Plane B, Plane C and so forth. Where the same competency was required for every job the company ever wanted to perform, that set of competencies becomes known as core competencies. Core competencies are the entry criteria to play in that market. Without the requisite of competencies the company does not get to first base. An example of a set of core competencies for a software company would include:

1 grand master and experts in system design;
2 experts in code generation;
3 experts in debugging;
4 grand master in systems testing;
5 expert in documentation and so forth.

If an organization becomes disjointed from its market you might hear a CEO ask 'Well what are your core competencies?'. In this way, by determining core competencies that are present, it might be possible to refocus the organization on market opportunities it had the competence and proficiency to pursue successfully. When organizations pursue this course of action it is usually because they have experienced some failure and there is a need to determine a new route to success. It's much harder to think your way out of this situation than its reverse, as here the company is saying 'What market problem do we have the competence to solve?'. Its reverse is more goal oriented – 'There is a problem in the marketplace and this is what we have to do to solve it'. The former is a solution looking for a question.

Planning for Capability and Proficiency

If an organization is looking to the future its CEO may ask 'If we want to win the contract to refurbish the cockpit of the X Plane what capabilities do we need to have in place?'. The response would be a dream ticket, but this time more specific to the job:

1 we need three experts in ergonomics;
2 we need three experts in instrumentation;
3 and so on.

Then by looking at the engineers the company employs it is possible to 'measure the gap' between competence, proficiency and the resulting capability. This is really useful as it tells the management of the company whether or not they can perform the contract if they win it. Of course they have to win the contract first – so the next question should be 'What capabilities do we have to have to win the X Plane contract?'.

If the result of the exercise reveals that the company has no experts, just one grand master and five competent performers, management can then decide what to do. One option would be to train the competent performers and make them into a team led by the grand master, hoping that they will become sufficiently proficient quickly enough under his tutelage. Option 2 might be to hire in some talent from outside the company. Option 3 is to scrap the idea of bidding for the contract at all!

┌─ KM Concept#15 ─────────────────────────────

Organizational Capability = Competence + Proficiency

Visualizing the Future

Pictures are always good things to use in analysing the ability of the company to offer a capability. The polar diagram in Figure 3.4 can be used to show how proficient a particular individual is. Let's say for example that Figure 3.4 represents a particular person. Actually this person is a well-rounded individual who is expert in most aspects of his particular job. The proficiencies in Figure 3.4 indicate where the person is in terms of development. This person is probably not a junior person. In general, to have eight dimensions each representing a competency the individual would have been working for several years. A graduate out of college for a couple of years may have four competencies they were working on. Figure 3.4 is useful as it permits us to compare an idealized person with a can-

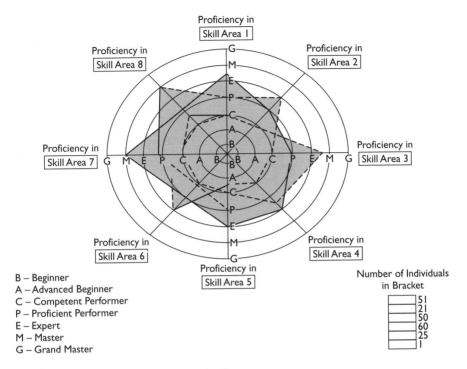

Figure 3.4 Proficiencies plotted on a polar diagram

didate for the job. If we had a polar diagram of every employee in the company who worked for us then when one left we might have a better idea of what we had lost. Then we could determine if the competency was core, critical and so forth.

On Track to Nowhere

One or two years ago a major railway research laboratory decided to create a database of all of the competencies possessed by its staff. The list of competencies ran to several hundred, and was flat, that is the competence was either present or absent. A typical example of a listing would be: 'Ability to design the simulation of a train crash' – three people. The exercise had been long, involving many people thinking about what their competencies were. But the exercise was also futile as in the end it didn't tell you anything about what proficiency the organization had, or more importantly what core competencies the laboratory needed to sustain its existence. In addition there was no indication of where the organization wanted to go. So a better exercise would have been to determine a set of goals. Draw up dream tickets to achieve each goal. Determine competencies, proficiencies and critical knowledge functions. Then look to see the size of the gap between where the organization wanted to go and its ability to get there.

4

Dimensions of Knowledge

Before a decision can be made to grow expertise organically or inorganically, more knowledge is needed about the nature of the missing knowledge – meta-knowledge. Meta-knowledge, helps us understand us how difficult the expertise would be to replace. The first aspect to examine is whether the required knowledge is tacit or explicit. This will give us a good indication whether or not the knowledge can be adequately learned by repeating a process which has been written down, or whether the acquisition of knowledge is more complex to understand and/or acquire.

EXPLICIT KNOWLEDGE

Explicit knowledge is knowledge which a person is able to make available to another for inspection. This may mean that it can be explained verbally, but it is generally preferable to codify it, that is, write it down. Types of

Figure 4.1 Explicit knowledge

explicit knowledge would include written explanations of business processes which have been written down in manuals or other documents. How to change the tyre on a car, or how to assemble a piece of furniture are examples of knowledge which has been made explicit and codified. A person with an appropriate background can follow the procedure and the result should be predictable and of a consistent quality. So a qualified mechanic should be able to follow a procedure to remove the engine from a car he or she has not worked on before, because he or she has the correct background to perform the task. A person who understands the rudiments of cookery should be able to follow a recipe he or she has not made before with a reasonable expectation of success.

Knowledge which has been documented in any form has been made explicit. So examples of explicit knowledge would include manuals, business processes, training material and so on. Of course having written knowledge does not necessarily mean that someone else can follow it with success (can you program your VCR?). But if the codification is a true representation of activity required to perform a task then an appropriately skilled person should be able to use it.

TACIT KNOWLEDGE

Tacit knowledge is knowledge which has not been made explicit. That may be for several reasons. Either the person who has the knowledge does not know how to convey it appropriately, or it may not be possible to convey it at all. Sometimes people don't know how they do something, and it may be necessary to find a way of externalizing tacit knowledge in order to make it explicit. One great way of really understanding what you know is to try to explain it to someone else, or even better teach someone else to do what you can do. This is fine when the task in hand is well understood, or you are teaching someone who is a peer. When there is a large gap between the teacher and student, say for example the teacher is a grand master and the student is a novice, there can be a communication gap between the two which is difficult to bridge. Recall two experts talking with each other, two mechanics, or two computer specialists. Do you understand what they are saying? Possibly not. That's because experts develop shortcuts over the years, or they just seem to 'know' what's wrong with a piece of equipment because of the way it looks, or sounds. They also talk in a language which manipulates concepts at a higher level of abstraction than the language in which novices communicate.

Where tacit knowledge can't be made explicit it may be because the knowledge is based upon the use of the senses. Take the instance where a

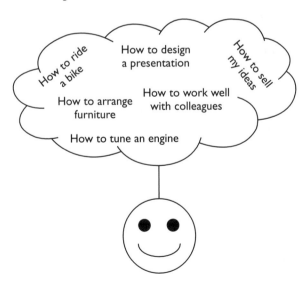

Figure 4.2 Tacit knowledge

designer is designing some new stationery for a customer or a new logo or advertisement. Asking them how they perform that task, and to perhaps write it down would be difficult for them. They would say 'It just looks right'. When a design satisfies some predetermined criteria it is finished, or good or whatever.

Another example might be a mechanic. An apprentice may be able to fix a car referring to manuals, but a grand master may 'know' the car is not right because of the sound of the engine. When the grand master tells the apprentice the car will be in balance when the engine 'sounds right' that message means nothing to the apprentice if he or she cannot recognize the 'right' sound.

MAKING KNOWLEDGE EXPLICIT GENERATES CORPORATE ASSETS

When a process is codified such that the knowledge can be transferred to other employees in written form it has been codified. As such it may then represent a business process or management procedure. Where knowledge is embedded within a procedure it becomes an infrastructure asset. This is desirable – if we refer back to the structure of intellectual capital, infrastructure assets are the assets which give the organization its strength to consistently perform tasks to achieve its goals. Where knowledge has not been codified it manifests as a human centred asset. The difference is important. As a human centred asset it belongs to the individual, as an infrastructure asset it belongs to the organization. The latter is desirable as it is easier to share knowledge which has been codified than it is to share knowledge which has not been codified.

Imagine a company at 10 am. Then imagine it at 10 pm. What's the difference? The difference is that as an empty building many knowledge assets will have gone home, gone scuba diving or gone off to become apprentice fire walkers (we actually had an employee who wanted to learn to be a fire walker – I discouraged it, but in reality had no control over the recreation time of this particular employee). The knowledge of the employee can (literally) go up in flames. This risk can be managed if knowledge can be documented and safely archived for the benefit of everyone else in the company. So the goal is to identify critical knowledge assets and where possible, and logical, codify them.

Explicit to Tacit

Just because knowledge is explicit does not mean that for every individual it stays so. Consider a situation where an apprentice learns to tune an engine. He (or she) will have attended classes and possibly taken exams where he may have been asked to write down a procedure for tuning an engine. In that event he may have used various measuring equipment to determine whether or not the engine was correctly tuned. Over the years he learns he can take short cuts when tuning an engine, and no longer uses the process he was taught at college. Now he has his own process which might not involve any specialist equipment at all. He uses his eyes and ears in place of monitoring equipment. His knowledge has become tacit. He has also moved up the scale of proficiency during that time and is now an expert. One day a new apprentice comes into the shop. The expert is asked to teach the lad how to tune an engine. The apprentice has no experience of what a tuned engine 'sounds like', and the expert has forgotten how to explain the tuning process in terms the apprentice can understand, even though he knows (or at least knew).

KM Concept#16

Making Knowledge Explicit Generates Infrastructure Assets

If the expert is asked to explain his short cuts to the apprentice and write them down he may not be able to. So the apprentice has to go through the same process as the expert in order to develop his or her own tacit understanding of the process.

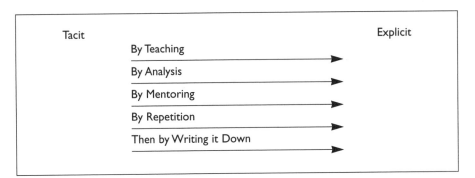

Figure 4.3 But it is not possible to make all tacit knowledge explicit

More Thinking about Knowledge

The study of knowledge and the development of a theory of knowledge – epistemology – has been discussed for many years, since the time of the ancient Greeks in fact. Here we are interested in the practical application of knowledge management within the organization. Once again I am borrowing another of Karl Wiig's useful paradigms for thinking about knowledge in the organization.

Levels of knowledge
- Goal setting or idealistic
  - vision, what's possible, goals, values.

- Systematic knowledge
  - problem solving strategies, general principles.
  - analysis strategies, reasoning ability.

- Pragmatic
  - factual knowledge.
  - decision making knowledge.

- Automatic
  - job related knowledge.
  - very familiar knowledge.

GOAL SETTING OR IDEALISTIC KNOWLEDGE

Idealistic knowledge would typically be found in a company leader or CEO. These people have a vision, and understand the basic principles of how to achieve it. What may be lacking is an understanding of management processes to move from A to B, but that's acceptable as long as this person surrounds him- or herself with others who can provide that function. This type of knowledge is in fact impotent unless it is supported by some of the other types of knowledge we describe below. In terms of tacit and explicit, a goal setter is likely to be analytic, able to explain an analytic process in the context of a corporate goal, so some of this knowledge will be explicit. That part associated with vision, opportunity and the future is tacit, and not necessarily well understood.

One interesting way in which this type of knowledge is demonstrated is in business plans which seek to raise venture finance. A visionary, such as the CEO of a new company, can 'see' a business and has a hypothesis of how to make a company and grow it into an organization as a result of taking advantage of the opportunity. In order to convince the venture capitalists to invest, the vision has to be described together with a rationale for the supporting plan. Getting the investor to share the vision is actually partly a sales job on the part of the new CEO, but explaining how and why the opportunity came about can be difficult if the CEO can't turn tacit knowledge into something explicit a venture capitalist can react to. Given this situation it's not surprising that venture capitalists are known for investing in people, people and people. It's not possible to validate a business opportunity which has yet to materialize with any real degree of certainty.

What to Do if Goal Setting or Idealistic Knowledge is Important

The first thing to do is to determine just how important this type of knowledge is. Once again the dream ticket method for projects that are underway should help to determine this. Some organizations require a number of individuals who can provide this type of knowledge on a regular basis. They may be project based organizations that require leadership or organizations that sell expertise and knowledge such as consulting houses. Hopefully every organization has at least one person at the head of the company who is able to provide this type of value. If the organization is not subject to a great deal of change this knowledge may not be important all the time.

Sadly it is difficult to teach people how to have vision, and how to be creative. It's possible to teach people methods to be more creative, but a process to make an uncreative person creative is a poor substitute for a born visionary and leader.

If this type of knowledge is critical the next step is to determine exactly who in the organization possesses it. There are a number of ways to do that which we will discuss later, but the most important point is to identify the individuals who appear to be able to provide vision, values, etc. and be nice to them so that they don't leave the company! That said a company with too many visionaries and multiple value systems is also a nightmare scenario, as it's probably impossible to get anything done.

┌─ KM Concept#17 ─────────────────────────────────┐
│   │
│   Goal Setting Knowledge Creates Dream Tickets │
│   │
└──┘

SYSTEMATIC KNOWLEDGE

Systematic knowledge is knowledge of how things get done. It includes problem solving strategies, knowledge of methodologies and so forth. This type of knowledge is essential to the competent working of any organization. People need to be able both to develop systems, methods and so forth, and then document them for others to use. This type of knowledge may start its life as tacit, when the method is an idea, or 'the way we did it last time'. ISO standards may be applied to aspects of systematic knowledge, which may lull the company into a false sense of security as the system itself may be inherently sub-optimal.

Problem solving strategies always fall into this category of knowledge, and occur in the situation where we find the 'emperor with no clothes on effect'. A problem which a group finds badly written is solved in minutes by someone else that has sound problem solving strategies. Once solved, the solution is obvious to the group. Such skills are displayed by analytic individuals, and psychometric tests can help identify individuals with this skill.

What to Do if Systematic Knowledge is Important

Once again, having people in the team who are good problem solvers is valuable, codifying the problem solving process is probably not of any general use to the organization. Teaching problem solving might be of use to raise the general competency of a group of individuals. Identifying problem solving methods for a specific problem and documenting them is wise in this instance as they may be transferable to another individual. In thinking about systematic knowledge it is necessary to try to understand how an individual goes about solving a particular problem. One way individuals perform a diagnosis is to quickly look at the symptoms of a situation and form a hypothesis. They then spend time attempting to disprove that hypothesis by gathering more data. Where the data support the hypothesis then the original diagnosis is determined to be accurate. Where the data do not support the hypothesis a new hypothesis needs to be found. Documenting this type of procedure where the domain is well defined can sometimes give novices the diagnostic abilities only previously afforded to grand masters, so depending upon the criticality of the situation it's worth thinking about.

MYCIN

Later we shall talk about expert systems, but this anecdote is a good example of a diagnostic process which had an unforeseen benefit. Several years ago some researchers decided to build a computer system which would be able to match the diagnostic expertise of an expert in the domain of bacterial infection. The resulting expert system was called MYCIN. The researchers worked with experts over a period of time and determined a sequence of events which led the expert to identify particular infections. A series of questions were asked by the computer system, something like the following:

Q: What is the patient's name?
A: John Doe
Q: Male or female?
A: Male
Q: Age?
A: 55
Q: Have you obtained positive cultures indicating general type?
A: Yes
Q: What type of infection is it?
A: Primary Bacterium
Q: When did symptoms first appear?
A: May 5
Q: Let's call the most recent positive culture CULTURE-1. From where was CULTURE-1 taken?
A: From the blood

MYCIN continues to quiz the doctor in this vein and eventually starts a line of questioning in preparation for prescribing a course of treatment. Approximately 500 'rules' constituted MYCIN's pool of knowledge about 100 causes of bacterial infection. When MYCIN was tested for accuracy of its diagnosis it was more accurate, more frequently than the doctors. However over a period of time the doctors became more and more accurate, which puzzled the researchers, until they discovered that the doctors had obtained a copy of the rules the computer was using, and by applying the same process their diagnostic performance had improved. By using the same deductive strategy as the expert system they themselves had exhibited 'expert performance'.

Pragmatic Knowledge

Pragmatic knowledge is factual knowledge and knowledge we use to make decisions. It is mostly explicit, well known and understood. This type of knowledge would represent the basic knowledge we have about everyday situations. If the traffic light is red – stop; if there is a car coming – don't cross the road; if you see a mad dog foaming at the mouth – don't pet it! This type of knowledge is well known and used conscientiously. When people do not appear to use pragmatic knowledge in a situation where we think they ought to, we tend to say that they have no common sense. Of course context is vital again, and maybe a 'smart' person can quickly apply pragmatic knowledge associated with one situation to another, and also explain their reasoning. Pragmatic knowledge in a work context would tend to represent fundamental acceptable behaviours. How processes are carried out on the factory floor, how an invoice is drawn up, how permission to travel is granted, etc.

What to Do if Pragmatic Knowledge is Important

Pragmatic knowledge will definitely be important within the organization. And as it is explicit it can be codified, that is written down. Not that we are suggesting that all pragmatic knowledge which the organization uses should be written down, because employees would spend so much time writing there would be no time left to work! So the important point is to determine whether pragmatic knowledge is critical or rare and then codify it. Where it is both critical and rare yet there is no time to spend on its codification it is important to understand in whose head such knowledge resides, and make sure that person does not leave the company.

Automatic Knowledge

Automatic knowledge is routine, working knowledge, and is mostly tacit. This is the type of knowledge which we use without thinking about it. The difficulty here is that it can be as insignificant as how to type on a keyboard, or as important as how to dynamite a bridge. The point is that the user of the knowledge just 'does things' without necessarily considering exactly why or how they are doing a particular task. Where the knowledge has become tacit this means it may be difficult for the individual to articulate. As we have already discussed that may be because the nature of the knowledge itself is really complex, or the individual has merely forgotten why he or she does what they do. Automatic knowledge is very familiar, and may be job related. Someone who performs a task over and over again has automatic knowledge.

What to Do if Automatic Knowledge is Important

If automatic knowledge is important in the organization, it is important to consider once again is it critical and is it rare? If knowledge is critical and rare, then the next issue is to determine whether or not it can be codified. If the nature of the knowledge is such that its owner cannot explain how a particular task is performed it will not be possible to codify it. If it's critical, rare and uncodifiable then it must be determined exactly how the individual came to be in possession of the knowledge. What was done in order to master it? What experiences did the individual have to reach that level of expertise? If this can be determined then a plan can be drawn up for another person to emulate the experience, and perhaps become an apprentice. Mentoring schemes can be used so that the apprentice 'grows' knowledge over a period of time by raising levels of competence and proficiency one after another. This type of scheme is known as organic, as the organization is 'growing its own'. If the knowledge is critical and there is no time to grow the expertise organically then the only solution is to import it from outside the organization, that is grow it inorganically. Inorganic growth has other difficulties associated with it, such as the cost of acquisition and issues associated with corporate culture which we will discuss later.

Critical and Rare?

By now it should be possible to recognize the danger signs, that is the situation where knowledge is critical and rare. Critical and rare knowledge is frequently found in the heads of individuals who have been working in the organization for a long time, and all of a sudden someone realizes that that individual is about to retire. Panic sets in – what is to be done? This situation is at least positive, as the organization *knows* that the knowledge is critical and rare. The really big problem arises when an organization is unaware that certain knowledge is critical and rare. The best way to work this out is to use the dream ticket method to determine if the knowledge is at least critical. If it is, then the next step is to see how prevalent it is within the organization. If it is widely prevalent then maybe it's not a problem. If all the knowledge is within one team then it's worth considering whether that team can leave as a whole. Financial trading houses sometimes have this worry, as a grand master in say Japanese investments may have a team of six working with him or her, and if a competitor wants to buy that expertise they can merely poach the entire team. In such a scenario the entire team is portable, they just resign and take up a new desk, doing exactly the same thing in another company. This can be a disaster, as not only does the original organization lose the competence and proficiency, they also lose all the market knowledge associated with the job function. It could take years to recover from such a loss.

If the knowledge is critical and rare the next step is to determine whether or not it is codifiable. If it's not codifiable action must be taken to replicate it organically or inorganically. If it is codifiable then the next step is to begin the process of knowledge elicitation, which is the subject of the next chapter.

KM Concept#18

Strive to Make Critical Knowledge Explicit

5

Capturing Knowledge Within the Organization

In this chapter we will look at the methods you will need to use if you decide to capture knowledge within the organization. In general we call these knowledge elicitation methods, as they refer to methods of eliciting knowledge from an individual. There are a variety of ways we can use but first there are some general principles.

About Verbal Reporting

When you talk to an individual and ask how he or she performs a task a communication medium must be found with which to do that. Options include talking to you, explaining what he or she does. Another way would be to draw a diagram. Most commonly people will talk back to you in response to a question. Verbalization which describes knowledge in some form, say a procedure, may not be accurate for a number of reasons, some of which the reporter may not even be aware of. When you ask people how a task is performed they will report introspectively. That is to say they will think about how they do something and report on *that* process. *That* process may not be what they actually do in their job of work – it's what they think they do during introspection. Now this is a reasonable starting point, but then the introspective process has to be validated in some way to determine if that's what they actually do in real life.

No Fat, No Future, No Revenue!

On one occasion we went to a manufacturing plant where margarine was invented. The management were worried that they were about to lose a really valuable skill. They had only two 'margarine men' who could invent low fat margarine. Both were in their late 50s. It seemed that the major problem was in knowing when the manufacturing process would successfully scale up. Huge quantities of margarine were thrown away after novices misjudged the process. Several attempts had been made to determine exactly what these two men knew, and how they could successfully predict when the process would scale up and when it would not. The organization had their margarine men interviewed, people had followed them around with clipboards trying to figure out what they did, consultants had been hired, all to no avail. We were supposed to be the experts in knowledge elicitation so off we went to meet the margarine men.

Clothed in white they were peering into a huge vat of margarine when we arrived. They welcomed us and and told us about how margarine was made. We taped it all, and took lots of notes. Eventually we got to the detail of the scaling up process and the conversation went something like this:

Annie: So how do you manage the scaling up process?
Margarine Man: Well, first we make a small container of margarine, say 20 gallons. Then if it looks right we make a bigger one. If it doesn't look right we throw it away and try again.
Annie: What do you mean 'looks right'?

Margarine Man: Well if the colour is right, we look at the sheen on the top of the mixture. If the sheen is right we listen to the way the paddles 'glop' as they move around.

Annie: But what about the taste?

Margarine Man: We stick our fingers into the vat and we taste it and maybe it needs some more emulsifier, or water, or salt, you know?

Annie: So if all this is fine then what? You make a bigger one and a bigger one? Then what?

Margarine Man: Yes, and if it looks right we keep going until we get to production size. If that doesn't look right we throw it away and try again.

Annie: Is that it? Don't you waste a lot of margarine?

Margarine Man: Oh yes. Tons of the stuff. But not as much as we used to.

They found the look of dismay on my face really entertaining. We knew we'd just become two more scalps to hang on their belt. We ruefully told the managers we could not help at all, but that they'd have to find an apprentice and permit him or her to make all the mistakes the experts had made – it was the only way.

KM Concept#19

Know Why Knowledge is Tacit

KNOWING WHAT YOU KNOW

Ask a colleague if he or she knows how to do something. The response is pondered. Does this colleague really know how to do something or just think he or she knows how to do it? A couple of years ago we had a colleague who had spent a great deal of time teaching various courses. He had worked for the company for several years, and was generally considered to be a 'bit of a star'. One of the seminars he taught was a marketing seminar on strategy which I had developed several years earlier called The Twenty Steps. The Twenty Steps led an individual through the process which is required in order to put a market strategy together, then validate it to make sure that there were no contradictions within the strategy. He had given this seminar many, many times. At one point we had a huge quantity of work which meant we needed this individual to work on the development of a marketing strategy for a fairly well defined market. Normally we would allow twenty man days for such a task. After a week or so some signs of strain were beginning to show as the individual blew open the market research, then had difficulty in getting his arms around the data and analysing it. However he was determined that he was doing fine and did not need any help. It got worse, and early drafts of pieces of the market overview made no sense at all. By the end of week two it was clear that there was no way he could complete the task without significant help from a more senior member of staff. Eventually the task was completed, but we destroyed an employee in the process as he really thought he could construct a marketing strategy on his own. He knew how to do it (he was competent), but he could not do it (he was not proficient). He left the company shortly afterwards in the mistaken belief that he had failed – he hadn't, he was just a novice when he thought he was an expert, and indeed we had failed to manage him properly through the learning process. The point here is that individuals will say that they can do something, perhaps when they think they can, or ought to be able to. Then later you might discover that they are not as proficient as they thought they were.

In the Heat of the Moment

Fifteen years ago some colleagues were conducting a study in preparation to build an expert system – a computer system that could perform a task in the same way a human performed it. The 'domain' for the study was the design of industrial heating and air conditioning. We had an expert we worked with who had designed air conditioning and heating systems for many years. The general idea was to have a series of interviews where an interviewer would work with an expert to try to determine how they go about their particular job. The interviews were taped so that the researchers could go over the tapes at a later date. During the first interview with our heating expert a discussion took place over where radiators would be placed in a room. The conversation went something like this:

> *Interviewer*: OK, so if you're designing central heating systems how do you decide where to put the radiators?
> *Expert*: Oh that's not a problem, you put them under the windows.

Interviewer: Why?

Expert: Because that's where they have to go.

Interviewer: (thinking the expert has failed to get the point of the exercise) Yes, but I know that *you* know that's where you have to put them, but if we wanted to build a computer system which would figure out where to put the radiators, how would it know where to put them?

Expert: (beginning to get irritated now) The computer would put the radiators under the window.

Interviewer: (now nervous that the expert is getting annoyed) But there must be a reason they are put under the windows, I have always thought this was odd as surely all the heat would just go out of the window wouldn't it?

Expert: (now annoyed) No the heat wouldn't go out of the window.

Interviewer: (now concerned the interview is going to become a catastrophe) OK, never mind. Perhaps we should look at a blueprint of a house, and you can tell me where you would like to put the radiators.

The interview was saved, but the expert was annoyed, and we were concerned that he would not agree to continue with the project. The next day he came back, full of smiles and apologies. He said 'I am really sorry about yesterday – you see I have been doing this for so long I had forgotten why the radiators always go under the windows, so I looked up my old college notes and of course there is an explanation. This is why . . .'

In this particular situation the expert was working at a higher level of granularity of knowledge than say an apprentice. This is quite common. When you are a novice you have to measure, take readings, and weigh things. When you are an expert you just 'know' where to put things, how much is the right quantity (did your grandmother use kitchen scales when she was baking or making a cake?). Although this type of knowledge is tacit it can be made explicit. But the explicit form of the knowledge may not reflect what the expert actually does. In trying to externalize the process the process itself has been changed. So in this case the computer system would either calculate where the radiators went or it could use some heuristics, or rules, as the expert had done. Such rules might include:

If there is a window in the room put the radiator underneath.

Frying Eggs

Sometimes it's a good idea to see if an individual is able to better explain his process by way of a diagram or written procedure. This can also be illuminating. Many years ago when I used to teach computer programming at college, it was the fashion to spend time teaching flow charting as a method for organizing the logic behind a process. During week 1 of flow charting it was always a good game to ask the class to construct a flow-chart called 'how to fry an egg'. Before assigning the task I would always say 'Is there anyone in this room who can't fry an egg?'. Following a response of much laughter – of course they can all fry eggs – the students began to construct their own chart. The chart is made up of process boxes which are rectangular, and decision boxes which have a yes or no answer. An example is shown in Figure 5.1. True to form, and excellent for entertainment value, every year we would have individuals who forgot to switch the cooker on, did not put oil in the pan, never switched the pan off and so forth. It's a great way of pointing out how much detail you

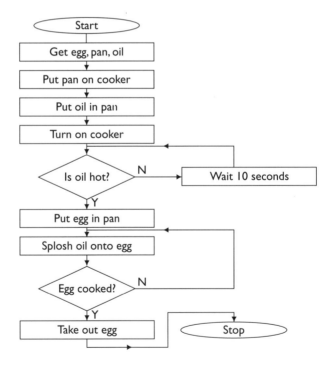

Figure 5.1 How to fry an egg

really need to pay attention to, even when the task is very simple, well understood and well defined. In every class I ever taught there were perhaps only one or two students who constructed an accurate chart for frying an egg.

Retrospective Reporting

When asking an individual to report on some activity he or she has the expertise to perform it may be useful to try to get an understanding of whether he or she is drawing on experiences stored away in long- or short-term memory, as the nature of retrospection will be different. If you ask a person who has just completed a task to report on it, then knowledge about that experience will be stored in short-term memory, and the report may not have much data on why certain outcomes were experienced. Interviewing someone who has recently performed a task will cause him or her to reflect further on the experience so then you may have some added value from asking questions how?, when?, why? If a person has performed that task some time ago the knowledge is stored in long-term memory, and it may be more difficult, and take longer for the individual to access. When debriefing a person or team after completion of some activity, most organizations, such as the military, choose to debrief a team as soon as possible after the task is concluded in order to access as much as possible before it is forgotten, or stored in long-term memory. Just because we have stored something in long-term memory does not mean that in future we will always be able to access it in a timely or accurate fashion.

METHODS FOR ELICITING KNOWLEDGE

There are several methods for eliciting knowledge which can be used in the workplace. These include:

1 questionnaires;
2 interviewing;
3 task in context analysis.

We will discuss the merits and appropriateness of each below.

Questionnaires

Questionnaires are useful when you want to survey knowledge or opinion in a broad based fashion. The difficulty with questionnaires is that if the question is not well constructed the questionnaire may not get the desired answer. Asking individuals to fill in questionnaires is universally disliked – perhaps it reminds us of being at school. It is curious how sometimes people change a verbal response from a written one. One curious discrepancy I have noted is between end of course 'wash out sessions' and the exit questionnaire. For a number of years we have taught a course at a client site in the UK on ways to leverage business from intellectual property. The course has a wash out session at the end where participants are encouraged to comment on the course, say what they did and did not like, make suggestions for improvements and so forth. They are also requested to fill out an exit questionnaire which is forwarded to the training department. Now it is clear that if you are silly enough to ask a group of smart scientists to comment on a two day course they have just completed you are going to get a lot of commentary. In our experience the commentary has mostly been complimentary. Yet on a number of occasions the exit questionnaires looked like they belonged to another course. Presenters were ranked as 1 or 2 out of 5, yet in discussion the same people would say – 'this was a great course'. Do people radically change their opinion and perception merely because they are asked to write it down? – it sounds unlikely, but it looks like it!

Questionnaires are a silver bullet approach. The questioner has one opportunity to get the question right. If the question is not answered properly or in enough detail the opportunity to probe for more detail is absent. So questionnaires are fine if the level of detail is not deep, the questionnaire unambiguous and the sample size large.

Interviews

Interviews are used when the interviewer wants the opportunity to probe, or wants to have an opportunity for a less structured approach to knowledge elicitation. It is recommended that some time is spent preparing for an interview, and that you have a guideline to follow, which might include a questionnaire. However in this context the questionnaire is used as the basis for managing the interview by the interviewer, and the goal is more likely to be to get the questions answered during the interview than to religiously follow the order of the questions. The questions are more like a guideline. Sometimes at the beginning it is a good idea to have several interview strategies and try them out to see which one yields the best results.

When interviewing an individual it is wise to get his or her permission to record the interview with an audiotape. Audio taping is a good idea because the interviewee quickly forgets that the tape is on and relaxes in to a style where communication is rich. Videotaping the interview is more obtrusive unless it can be done from another room. The real benefit of audio taping is that during the interview the major job of the interviewer is to keep the conversation flowing in the right direction. Frequently there is no time for the interviewer to synthesize the responses of the interviewee. The audio tape allows the interviewer and colleagues to ponder over the tape at their leisure at a future time. Another benefit is that note taking is not quite so important as everything is recorded.

Not a Spanish Inquisition

In order to get a relaxed and quality interview the interviewer needs to bond with the interviewee. So if there are several people interested in participating in the interview process only one should actually conduct the interview (Figure 5.2). Our favourite method is to have observers arranged in the room so that they are not in direct view of the interviewee, who is seated at right angles to the interviewer. Having observers is a good idea as during the interview the interviewer may not pursue a line

Figure 5.2 The knowledge elicitation team

of questioning which they should have taken. Observers can take a note of that, and at the end of the interview the interviewer can then draw the interviewees' attention to the observers and open up the discussion to include them, one at a time, with an opening like 'does anyone have any questions (I should have brought up and didn't)?'. Then one by one each can ask their questions. It's important not to have the interviewee facing a panel who grill them. It's also important that one person forms a really good relationship with the interviewee.

On one occasion we interviewed a scientist who for some reason whenever asked a question by a woman, directed his answer to a male in the room, presumably because they thought the males understood the answer better! No matter, if man to man is the way to get the best quality interview, change roles and make it happen.

It's worth spending a couple of minutes on the male/female phenomenon here. A well handled interview can be a very positive experience for the interviewee, who is frequently flattered by the attention. After all, it's nice to be told you are special and valuable and to ask someone to talk for a couple of hours about themselves. In general we have observed from many hundreds of interviews with experts that both men and women respond better to a female interviewer. We suspect the reason for this is that men are less threatened by a female interviewer and women find a female interviewer more sympathetic. So it is our preference to use very smart young females who cannot only track the discourse, but also show sympathy to the interviewee.

┌─ KM Concept#20 ─────────────────────────────┐
│   │
│   Know Where Deep Knowledge Needs to be Captured │
│   │
└───┘

What a Little Gem You Are!

Around about the same time as we were conducting the study with the heating expert I visited my parents who live in Australia. My mother is a gemmologist. She can identify a huge range of gemstones and value them. She also looks at uncut stone, decides if it is worth cutting, where to cut it and so forth. So I thought it would be interesting to see what her process was when she identified stones. She agreed to be a guinea pig. So we sat down in the kitchen – me with my tape recorder, she with some stones.

Annie: What is the first thing you do when you look at a stone?

Mum: Well the most important things to look for in a stone are colour, clarity and brilliance.

Annie: OK, so what's this one?

Mum: (looking at the stone through her special spy glass) That's an aquamarine, and it's a beauty, look at its colour.

Annie: How much do you think its worth?

Mum: (fiddling with the stone, holding it between her thumb and index finger) It's probably worth about four hundred bucks.

Annie: How do you know it's not a sapphire, a pale sapphire could look like that couldn't it?

Mum: (with emphasis in her voice) Because it's not a sapphire, it's an aquamarine!!

Annie: Yes, I know it's not a sapphire, but how do you know?

Mum: (looking at her stupid daughter) Because the readings on the refractometer for a sapphire and an aquamarine are different.

Annie: Yes, but you're not using a refractometer, we don't even have one in the house, so how do you know?

Mum: Because I went to college for four years to understand how to do this. *Anne*, I'm an expert!

At this point I decided to make a pot of tea. The British always make tea in a crisis.

With a large sigh, my mother cleared up her stuff, and announced that my tape of her analysis activity was useless, she would only continue with the experiment if she could make her own tape. I agreed (eventually one learns about these things). The next day after poring over her books and various bits of equipment, she slapped a tape into my hand and announced, 'That's what I do'. The tape was a classic textbook procedure for identification of stone. A procedure she had not bothered to follow for more than 10 years.

This situation is a bit more difficult, as there are many visual skills involved in looking at stones. What is a 'beautiful colour' to her is not to me. In the context of aquamarines her judgement of 'a beautiful' colour is exact. I'm just comparing it to a colour I like. To train to be a gemmologist you have to look at a lot of stones, good and bad, in order to be able to recognize good. This type of knowledge is tacit and extremely difficult to convey from one person to another without some form of 'apprenticeship' looking at good and bad. (I'll spare you our conversations on the lustre of pearls!)

Dos and Don'ts in the Interview Process

There are a number of rules which should be adhered to when interviewing. Don't ever directly challenge an interviewee on a point of accuracy unless you have built up a relationship of mutual trust and respect. A mistake like this in the early stages of interview can alienate an interviewee permanently.

Another don't is to get involved in sharing your opinions with the interviewee. The point of the interview is to elicit their knowledge not demonstrate yours. The duration of an interview should not be more than a couple of hours at a time. Time will fly if the interview is going well, but to keep both interviewer and interviewee rooted in a chair for any longer is counterproductive. Our experience tells us that an interviewer cannot cope with more than 4 hours of interviewing a day. When we have attempted three 2 hour interviews in one day the interviewers are exhausted.

Finally be positive at all times. Give lots of positive feedback to the interviewee, smile, nod, make noises, etc. to let him or her know that things are moving along nicely.

Should Experts Interview Experts?

This is an interesting question as many people think that someone who is not versed in a particular domain cannot possibly interview an expert. Actually this is not the case at all, and in fact I think not being an expert in the domain is an advantage sometimes. If you listen to two experts talking with each other they always talk about exchanging information at a higher level of granularity than two novices or two apprentices. When two experts talk they tend not to challenge all sorts of things, probably out of deference for each other. When you want to get down to the nitty gritty of a situation it's best to challenge almost everything. That means it is important to be able to ask the 'stupid' questions. Experts don't tend to ask stupid questions of each other. But it's alright for a novice to ask stupid questions, and so frequently we find that it's as a result of these innocent questions that huge revelations come about. The expert might reply: 'I never thought about that', 'yes you could do A instead of B' and so forth. That is not to say that an idiot can be an interviewer: interviewers need to be mentally agile, and pick things up on the fly, but just enough to formulate the next question. Do they have to understand every answer the expert gives? No, because the support team can unravel the answers later, but the interviewer must be able to understand enough of the conversation in order to keep the knowledge elicitation process flowing.

Probing

When eliciting knowledge verbally, as experienced in an interview, sometimes there is a need to probe for a more in-depth answer to a particular question. Probing is an art, and how it is used will depend on the nature of the response the interviewer is seeking. If the interviewer wants to know about generalities, or they are interested in understanding the thinking that went on behind a particular process they may use undirected probes such as: 'Tell me more about that'; 'Can you give me a bit more detail?'; 'What were you thinking when you did that?'.

Sometimes a specific probe is not really necessary, yet a response is required, in which case an interviewer may merely nod at the interviewee, make positive noises such as 'Hmmm', or 'That's interesting', 'How clever' and so on. On other occasions probing may need to be direct such as 'Tell me exactly what you did to determine it was an X'.

The art in probing is to make sure that the interview never gets off track, or is diverted because the interviewer and interviewee are having a good time. Sometimes it will be necessary to probe directly, sometimes to focus on direct probing too soon means the interviewer fails to get insight into the big picture.

Modalities

Modality refers to the context in which the knowledge which is elicited is expected to be used. Take for example an expert who is diagnosing blood diseases. We can desire to elicit his or her knowledge in order to get someone else to perform the same task or we can desire the knowledge to teach someone else to perform the task. There is a difference, and that difference is in the extent to which every decision needs to be able to be justified. When you are working with an expert you don't ask him or her to justify every decision he or she makes, you just assume that because this person is an expert he or she knows what he or she is doing. If you are acting as a teacher then it is acceptable to have your every decision questioned. So if the purpose of knowledge elicitation is to teach someone else then the modality of the knowledge has to support education. If the purpose is to elicit knowledge just to perform the task (almost in dumb mode), then the modality of the knowledge has to support performing an expert task. The nature of modality will tell the interviewer the depth of knowledge which has to be gleaned in order to satisfy the requirement, and the extent to which it is able to be explained.

Modalities
Modes of expertise

- Domain: GEM identification
- Mode 1: To identify
- Mode 2: To teach to identify
- Mode 3: To validate identification
- Mode 4: To explain identification process

Task in Context Analysis

This process is used where you observe an individual performing a particular task, observing the method and so forth. The purpose is typically to see if the process is optimal, then suggest ways of improving it. I suppose this is not very different from time and motion study as it used to be called some 30 years ago. Sometimes the reasons for activity may not be obvious, so the interviewer may ask the individual to report on what he or she is doing as he or she performs the task. However self-reporting whilst performing a task is unnatural for a proficient person, so as the outsider you have interfered with the way the task is being performed.

If you ask someone who is tuning an engine to verbalize while tuning the engine you have changed the task. As the new task is tune the engine, verbalizing what you are doing, which is different from tuning the engine. So in reality you may still not get a real idea of what the individual is doing. Sometimes individuals do something that they cannot explain, which may be because they don't know how to explain what they are doing, they've forgotten, or perhaps they've been told to do it and never questioned why.

CONCLUSIONS

During this chapter we have discussed some of the ways in which to begin to gather information, data and knowledge from individuals, and you can see that it can be a fairly laborious process. Over the years computers have automated some of these processes, primarily as early prototyping vehicles for expert systems. In the next chapter we will discuss the tools which you can use in order to aid in the knowledge management process.

KM Concept#21

Know How to Elicit Knowledge

6

Aspects of Corporate Memory

One of the things to consider before embarking on a knowledge elicitation exercise is how the knowledge is going to be stored in the organization, that is the physical mechanism which is going to be used to store it. There are several options which we will consider:

- documents;
- documents in document management systems;
- in groupware such as Lotus Notes;
- in expert or knowledge based systems.

The decision to choose a particular mechanism will depend on several criteria which we will discuss before we look at various 'storage and retrieval' options.

1 The modality of the knowledge.
2 The longevity of the knowledge.

3 The extent to which the knowledge will grow and change.

4 The mechanism for managing the maintenance of the knowledge.

5 The return on investment required from putting the knowledge into some form of system.

6 The size of the problem space to which the knowledge has to be applied.

7 The complexity of the problem which the knowledge addresses.

8 The number of people who wish to have access to the knowledge.

9 The location of the people who wish to have access to the knowledge.

10 The sensitivity and confidentiality of the knowledge.

11 Whether the knowledge has to be guarded or protected.

12 Whether the knowledge is expected to grow without human intervention.

13 The nature of the knowledge.

1 THE MODALITY OF THE KNOWLEDGE

The modality of the knowledge refers to the way in which the knowledge will be used. For example will the knowledge be used to tell someone how to clean out a boiler, or will it be used to teach someone how to clean out a boiler, is the knowledge emulating an expert or a novice, under what circumstances, say mission critical, is the knowledge expected to perform and so forth? The modality will have impact on the depth of knowledge which needs to be gathered, accuracy and so forth.

If knowledge is going to be used to teach someone who requires to pick up a new competency then it is going to be necessary to ensure that the knowledge is represented at the appropriate level of granularity. The user profile will also have an impact on how knowledge is presented. For example if the knowledge is to be used to advise on activity during the meltdown of a nuclear reactor then before beginning the knowledge acquisition process it would be necessary to build a model of expertise of the user. If the user is a novice, he or she will require knowledge to be presented at a level of granularity that is considerably coarser than an expert who would require knowledge at a finer granularity. It's back to how best to communicate to a person, as a novice or an expert.

If the knowledge is to be used to teach a competency, then it would need to also have some feature which would allow the learner to ask questions such as why?, when?, how? However it would be tedious to assume that every student will want everything explained in detail every time they use the knowledge, as over a period of time their competence will grow. As competence grows the user will want the knowledge presented in a more convenient format.

```
┌─ KM Concept#22 ─────────────────────────────────────────────┐
│                                                              │
│        Know What Modality Knowledge Will Be Used For         │
│                                                              │
└──────────────────────────────────────────────────────────────┘
```

2 THE LONGEVITY OF THE KNOWLEDGE

The longevity of the knowledge refers to the length of time it is expected that the knowledge will 'live' for. This is a tough one, as one of the ways innovation occurs in the organization is by applying knowledge that was generated in one particular domain to another. If you consider a situation where a group of engineers might want to remove the wings from plane A, and they do not know how to do it, but do have a process to remove the wings from plane B, then they might choose to follow the procedure for plane A until it broke, then modify the process to deal with the peculiarities of plane B. We always advise our clients to assume that any knowledge captured might have a life of 20 years. It is interesting to speculate on knowledge relating to computer code as we near the year 2000. This is a long time, but it does at least ensure that the mechanism chosen for storage and retrieval will not have to be changed several times because no one could predict what the knowledge would be used for in the future. Just recently I learnt that code written for the IBM 701 was being converted to cope with date changes for the year 2000. The code was written in 1951. The computer software and knowledge of the code is 50 years old, and still going strong!

The 5,000 Year Know-How of the Iceman

In Europe we have become quite concerned in recent years over 'lost crafts', such as beer making or thatching roofs. Perhaps the longest living knowledge I have come across recently has been how shepherds move their flocks from low to high ground in the summer. Recent studies of the Iceman found in 1991 in the Tyrolean mountains indicate that some 5,000 years ago, that was exactly what he was doing when he got caught in a freak snow storm and died, becoming mummified in the ice. Years of speculation by anthropologists concerning exactly what the Iceman was doing up in the mountains when he died were never taken seriously by local Tyrolean shepherds who knew perfectly well what he was doing as they still do it today! The only difference is that today they use a trail which was made with dynamite about a hundred years ago. Surprise, surprise, before that trail was constructed they used one which passed exactly by the spot where the Iceman was discovered.

3 THE EXTENT TO WHICH THE KNOWLEDGE WILL GROW AND CHANGE

The extent to which knowledge will grow and change will have an impact on how it is stored and retrieved. If the knowledge is static then it's acceptable to put it into some serial storage mechanism such as a book or document. If the knowledge needs to be changed frequently, rewriting parts of physical documents, such as books, is time consuming and expensive. Consider highly dynamic knowledge such as knowledge about movements of stocks and shares. The mechanism has to mirror the requirement.

KM Concept#23

Know How Dynamic Knowledge Is

---

4 THE MECHANISM FOR MANAGING THE MAINTENANCE OF THE KNOWLEDGE

If the knowledge under consideration is volatile, that is it will change considerably over a period of time then the way in which it will be maintained needs to be considered before its storage mechanism is determined. Who will be responsible for maintaining up to date knowledge? How will they do it? Where will they get it from? How will its validity be ensured, and most importantly what will motivate them to do it? Answers to these questions will have a bearing on the eventual mechanism which is used to store and retrieve knowledge.

5 THE RETURN ON INVESTMENT REQUIRED FROM PUTTING THE KNOWLEDGE INTO SOME FORM OF SYSTEM

The return on investment will have an impact on the type of knowledge system which is deployed. In this case some expectation of impact must be defined, then a method of measuring that impact needs to be determined. Take the example of an army unit whose function is to maintain railway track. It seems that in the USA the army maintains a huge quantity of track, and in many cases when faults with the track occur, the event which caused the fault is the geology of the area, not the track, trains and so forth. Assigning a geological specialist to every track maintenance team is expensive, and that expense can be measured in terms of a man–day cost. So it was decided to build a small system on a computer which would ask the engineers questions about the terrain. Their answers were yes/no answers, which would lead them down a path eliminating various solutions as it went along, resulting in the definition of a problem and a set of actions to be taken to alleviate the problem. This was actually a small expert system which had been deployed on a portable computer. The keyboard had been covered up with a bigger keyboard which only had a small number of keys: START, STOP, YES, NO. The system was actually quite expensive to build as it required an in-depth elicitation exercise with a geologist experienced in railway track. After a period of time the soldiers stopped using the system, as they had learnt to recognize the symptoms of the most common geological problems. In this case the ROI would need to include the cost of building and deploying the system, against either the cost of teaching the soldiers in the classroom and/or the cost of putting a geological expert on every railway maintenance team.

6 The Size of the Problem Space to which the Knowledge has to be Applied

If the size of the problem space is small then it may be appropriate to write procedures down on cards or in manuals. If the problem space is large then this may not be practical. Consider a company that manufactures helicopters. When a helicopter is delivered to a client a truckload of manuals also needs to be sent. In this case procedural knowledge that could be stored in a computer system would mean sending a few CDs. Even so this is still too large and complex a domain for a maintenance engineer to wade through. So now companies that manufacture equipment which represents locating knowledge in a large problem space are designing intelligent manuals, that can converse with the user and assist them to locate the data, information and knowledge they require. In addition the system learns about the person who is using it, so it has a notion of the level of competence of the individual, and treats him or her accordingly.

7 The Complexity of the Problem which the Knowledge Addresses

The complexity of the problem the knowledge contributes to solving will determine whether the 'solution' can be found in one place, or the mechanism required needs to be able to look in multiple places at the same time. This might be the case when a consulting house with a global practice has an employee who wants to find out if anyone in the organization has worked with Mexican oil rigs before. If the consultant is based in Mexico, someone else with that knowledge might be based in Australia. In that case the mechanism which would need to be deployed must be able to search some form of knowledge base which was distributed over multiple geographies.

KM Concept#24

Know Who Needs to Know What in the Organization

8 The Number of People who Wish to have Access to the Knowledge

The number of people needing access to knowledge in the organization will have an impact on the mechanism which is used to deploy the knowledge. If all employees are required to use the corporate memory, then a suitable mechanism has to be found so that they can. If the variety and quantity of knowledge is substantial this might indicate that access should be via a computer, and in that case the mechanism would indicate that every employee needs to have a computer on his or her desk.

9 The Location of the People who Wish to have Access to the Knowledge

The location of the people who wish to access the knowledge is also important. Are they in offices, are they at the bottom of the sea, or even on the moon? Are they located as a group in one place or are they located in a group which is spread all over the globe? The location will also have a bearing on the concurrency of the group, that is their desired ability to act as a team simultaneously when they are in different time zones – maybe half the team is in bed while the other half are at their desks!

10 The Sensitivity and Confidentiality of the Knowledge

Sensitivity and confidentiality is a key issue for some companies. Consider a situation where knowledge of a market or situation turns out to be a competitive advantage. If knowledge is to be stored in some form of computer system, then perhaps it needs to be password protected, or perhaps even encrypted as it is moved from one location to another. It all depends on the nature of the knowledge which is put into the corporate memory.

11 WHETHER THE KNOWLEDGE HAS TO BE GUARDED OR PROTECTED

Knowledge can be protected as a form of intellectual property in some cases. If knowledge is a trade secret then some acknowledgement from the person who is accessing the knowledge is required before it can be shared. Then an agreement needs to be put in place to do that. If the knowledge is in the form of some kind of process then the organization might be interested in patenting it. Once again indiscriminate sharing of knowledge outside the organization might result in disclosure which could prevent a patent from being registered at a later date, as the knowledge could be deemed to be in the public domain.

12 WHETHER THE KNOWLEDGE IS EXPECTED TO GROW WITHOUT HUMAN INTERVENTION

In some cases systems can be built which have a capability to learn over a period of time without human intervention. Take for example a credit card system that keeps and grows knowledge about its customer base. Over a period of time it has monitored the spending of its customers. Certain customers have certain spending profiles which have been observed by the computer, then 'learnt'. If a customer suddenly displays some spending behaviour which is atypical then the system thinks 'This person's credit card is being used by someone else – I won't authorize this transaction until I can have the identity of the customer verified'. In this case perhaps the store assistant has to make a phone call to the credit authorization company who, with access to the customer account, asks the customer where they had lunch last Tuesday (assuming they billed it to the card!).

13 THE NATURE OF THE KNOWLEDGE

Finally of course there is the nature of the knowledge itself. There are the physical attributes of the way the knowledge is stored. Is it stored as bits or atoms? Bits means it has been digitized, and can therefore be manipulated by computer. If it is recorded as atoms, say written on stone, or as an oil painting then it cannot be manipulated by computer (unless you photograph or scan it first!). Then there is the type of knowledge which has not been externalized in the outside world in any way, such as the knowledge of what makes a garden beautiful, or margarine taste good – it's tacit.

Another dimension is the type of knowledge which you desire to keep and manipulate. Is it anecdotal knowledge of customer accounts? Is it knowledge about individuals such as their psychometric profiles which you may want to display as graphics and charts? Is it a video or a lecture which has been recorded?

Documents

Recording knowledge in documents is perhaps the most common method of keeping knowledge which can be codified. Examples would include books, manuals, etc. and also, these days, electronic documents. If knowledge is recorded in electronic form and then printed, changing it from bits to atoms, then problems will occur if the nature of the knowledge is volatile. Naturally this is the case more frequently than one might imagine even for systems assumed to be stable, such as manuals about maintaining aircraft that have been in use for 20 years. The issue is that despite the fact that the aircraft itself might be stable, the knowledge relating to it may grow constantly. Technological advances might change the way in which particular maintenance procedures take place. The body of knowledge concerning the craft may grow over time as individuals learn new short cuts, or new ways to identify problems.

When to Record Knowledge as Documents

Knowledge can be recorded as documents in electronic format and modified *ad infinitum*. Indeed there are some sophisticated document management systems which are able to manage that process effectively. If the nature of the knowledge in the document changes frequently then the document management system would need to have a change control mechanism so that individuals would know which version they were working with. Where documents are produced by teams of people, such as a set of helicopter maintenance manuals, document management systems ensure that concurrent workers are able to contribute to the same document simultaneously.

Writing knowledge down is one of the skills which has provided the foundation for our civilization, and regardless of whether we write by chipping symbols into stone or write by typing into a computer I expect we will continue the habit. When to capture knowledge by writing it down and when not to is a difficult question because we are unable to predict the future, and therefore unable to predict a future demand for something we have written today. Assuming that knowledge is codifiable it is worth documenting it if:

1 it is rare;
2 it represents a critical knowledge function;
3 it is new.

Is Document Management Knowledge Management?

No. Document management manages the life cycle of production, modification and maintenance to a document. Because documents can be searched in a variety of ways it is true that you can gain access to the information on a document more easily than otherwise. But documents only represent a particular aspect of knowledge which we would expect to find in corporate memory – knowledge that has been written down in the form of documents. Where it is inappropriate or impossible to do that the knowledge is missing from the document management system.

THE BENEFITS OF COMPUTERS TO KNOWLEDGE MANAGEMENT

Computers bring a number of benefits when using them as the mechanism for managing knowledge. First computers can provide 24 hour-a-day access to employees anywhere in the world who have access to a computer and possibly a telephone from which they can gain access remotely. Second computers can support multiple users simultaneously – so theoretically one expert system can advise thousands and thousands of doctors simultaneously. Computer systems can also be designed to automatically pick up data from external sources such as the stock market, and modify their behaviour in real time, that is, instantaneously as the situation is changing. Where information, data and knowledge are incomplete computers can be programmed to work with what they have, refining a diagnosis over a period of time as more and more data and information become available.

Where knowledge is kept as bits instead of atoms, modification is easy and instantaneous. Keeping data, information and knowledge digitized makes it much easier to manage it. The distribution of knowledge is faster and less time consuming if it is kept digitally. What used to be represented as a truckload of manuals, can now be sent directly to the user either down the telephone line, or by mail in a much more convenient format such as a series of compact discs.

Recording Knowledge in Groupware

Some organizations are using groupware to share knowledge about how to perform a particular job, or anecdotal material concerning customer accounts. Groupware applications can be searched for keywords which will track down a 'note' in the system. However, like document management systems the knowledge has to be codifiable, that is written down. There is no doubt that groupware applications have made a huge contribution to the sharing of knowledge that it is possible to write down, but like document management systems they provide no solution to the management of knowledge which is either too expensive to codify, not codifiable, or there is simply not enough time to codify it. Basically, today, groupware applications cannot provide the infrastructure for the comprehensive knowledge management infrastructure in a company – the corporate memory.

Artificial Intelligence, Mother of Computer Science

Computer scientists have always been interested in seeing if the computer can be used as a tool not only to emulate, but to synthesize human behaviour. The area of research became known as artificial intelligence, and researchers are comprised not only of computer specialists but also psychologists, linguists and philosophers. Because artificial intelligence always pushed the frontiers of computer science it has had many children over the years. Real time systems, the entire area of object orientation, multimedia, and even the basis for Microsoft Windows are all derived from research initially undertaken as artificial intelligence.

When we look back to the late 1960s researchers in Artificial Intelligence were trying to build machines that could solve general problems like how to navigate around a room in the same way as a human would. For those of you who are thinking that artificial intelligence was a failure, try constructing a flowchart to navigate around a room as an intelligent vacuum cleaner. This problem is enormously complex. How does a vacuum cleaner know what is garbage on the floor to be picked up or vacuumed around? What's a piece of furniture? How do you make a plan to get around it? Of course as humans we have automatic knowledge which we use to navigate around a room, computers have to be taught to do this, and taught to recognize all the elements which make up a room. The problem space is very large. Sadly that's why we don't have intelligent vacuum cleaners yet.

BUILDING MODELS

During the early phases of knowledge elicitation the interviewer and the team will begin to form some opinion on how the expert is performing a specific task. Perhaps they have some idea of a model of expertise or behaviour that the individual has. The extent to which a detailed model of human expertise will be required depends upon what the knowledge is intended to be used for. If the primary goal is to identify a procedure that an individual goes through in order to diagnose a fault in some machinery, they may go through some hypothesis testing. This means that based on a cursory overview of a situation an engineer may develop a hypothesis, then spend the rest of the time attempting to disprove it. If that's what he does then the process should try to demonstrate the same method. Where these processes are complex, and the resulting decision making criteria and method are complex it may be appropriate to build an expert system.

Expert Systems

One way of making the computer system more effective in solving problems is to limit the problem space and the domain – the world in which the computer is expected to operate. The general problem solving programmes built in the 1960s lived in the same world we did, even having to cope with gravity. By limiting the domain to a smaller world for example the world of identifying bacterial blood, the computer has a much better chance of being able to perform with a competence similar to that of a human being. So using computers as advisors, teachers and repositories of knowledge in limited domains is something to consider if the benefits of computerization are useful to the knowledge dissemination process. Of course this is also highly dependent upon the nature of the problem to be solved. If the problem requires the manipulation of knowledge such as that of the margarine men or the gemmologist the computer won't fare very well, as giving computers the vision capabilities of a human is a challenge we still have to face.

KM Concept#25

Use Expert Systems to Capture Deep Knowledge

The Architecture of Expert Systems

Expert systems are different from other types of computer system because of the way in which they work. One benefit of the architecture is that it is easier to add new knowledge to the systems without incurring the risk of upsetting the control flow of the software as so frequently happens with conventional software.

Expert systems are comprised of four components: a knowledge base, an inference engine, the explanation feature and a user interface. The knowledge base is normally constructed of facts and rules similar to the type already referred to with MYCIN. Facts are short-term information perhaps relating to a problem which the system is trying to solve, perhaps details of the terrain where the railway track has broken. The rules in the knowledge base can be quite simple and may be constructed as an IF . . . THEN pair referred to a production rule.

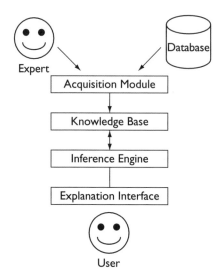

Figure 6.1 Architecture of an expert system

An example of rules to make French dressing might include:

IF the dressing needs to be sharp THEN the vinegar should be twice the volume of the oil

IF the dressing needs to be mild THEN the vinegar should be in equal proportions to the oil

and facts might be:

For every 250mls of vinegar add one teaspoon of sugar, half a teaspoon of salt and one table spoon of mustard.

Rules are triggered when they represent a true situation. So for example if a rule were:

IF the temperature is 35 degrees THEN turn on the air conditioning

when the temperature did reach that heat the computer would turn on the air conditioning. The mechanism which constantly looks at the rule base is the inference mechanism. The inference mechanism loops around the knowledge base, constantly looking to see if some new data have been received which might trigger one of the rules.

If the user wants to have an explanation for how and why the system came to a particular conclusion, the user can invoke the explanation feature. This feature gives the user the rationale for its conclusion by showing the various rules which were triggered, providing a tracking mechanism for the logic it used to come to a conclusion.

An interesting attribute of the knowledge base is that rules are not necessarily connected procedurally to each other. That means you can swap the order of them around and it won't have any impact on the performance of the system. The inference mechanism does not care which order the rules are in as it constantly searches the rule base over and over again looking to see if new data have arrived to trigger a rule.

Another convenient attribute of this type of system is that the rule base can grow over a period of time. As new knowledge is discovered it can be input to the system as a new set of rules. So over a period of time the system can become better and better.

This is a very superficial introduction to the concept of expert systems; there are many books on the subject for those who would like to understand how to build them in more detail. However it is also possible to buy expert system shells, which are off the shelf software products whose function is to provide the software infrastructure for an expert system. Just as when you first begin to build a database you buy the software from say FileMaker or an Oracle database that lets you populate the software, that is input records, modify them and change them. An expert system shell provides the infrastructure to input knowledge and modify it. Then after inputting data and information about a problem which needs a solution the inference mechanism looks to see if there are a set of rules which would enable the system to solve the problem.

Knowledge Engineering

By now you might have wondered how the rules are constructed. The process of unravelling unstructured knowledge from the interview process and codifying it into a set of rules is called knowledge engineering. The knowledge engineer is looking to represent the knowledge which has been elicited from the expert into a format required by the expert system. Also knowledge engineers may decide not to use an off the shelf expert system shell but construct a system of their own whose architecture best suits the problem domain. It really depends on how complex the problem and domain are.

When to Use Expert Systems

First expert systems are a type of software, so all the benefits of using computers can be applied to expert systems. Depending upon the domain it may take many man years of effort to build an expert system so the investment must justify the return. If the knowledge which is to be captured is rare, and its wide exposure might be considered a corporate advantage it may make sense to build an expert system. Many have concluded that the explanation feature of the expert system enables it to act as a teacher of sorts. In reality the explanation feature is serendipitous with regard to an educational instrument, and should be used to ensure that the conclusion the system came to can be validated by a human if necessary. The educational benefits of expert systems are limited compared to computer systems which have been specially designed to teach, but it is true to say that the competence of some individuals has been improved as a result of having a framework to both apply rules and understand how and when they are triggered.

7

Generating Knowledge within the Organization

If a decision is made to manage knowledge within the organization it's worth spending some time considering how and where knowledge is generated in the work environment, and also to look at the ways it is passed from one person to another (or not!).

Knowledge is generated as a by-product of several types of interaction some of which are listed below, and then briefly discussed.

1 As a product of experience (on the job).
2 By importing know-how with people.
3 As a product of a mentoring programme.
4 As a product of certain types of education and training.
5 By generating new knowledge through analysis.

6 Through interaction with outside agents.
7 Through brainstorming.
8 By talking!
9 By teaching.
10 By listening to your intuition.

1 As a Product of Experience (on the job)

Most people find learning by doing one of the best ways of creating new knowledge. The only drawback to this is the balance between doing something and knowing why you are doing it. Maybe that matters or maybe it doesn't. If there is a maintenance procedure which needs to be carried out and an apprentice has learnt how to perform it, everything will work if all the right tools are there, and all the right resources such as oils, fluids, filters and so forth. What happens if there is no oil? The apprentice may merely conclude that the maintenance procedure cannot be completed until the resource is replaced. The master may decide to make up an oil as a stop gap procedure. Herein lies the difference between various levels of knowledge. So within the organization that you work in, it will be necessary to determine whether or not on the job learning needs to be reinforced with an education programme which provides answers to the 'Why?' questions. As in most things balance is everything and the extent to which the workforce is truly knowledgeable and proficient will depend upon the situation.

2 By Importing Know-How with People

Sometimes there just isn't time to develop staff organically, that is growing staff who are already employed within the company by way of training, apprenticeship and so on. In this case the answer may be to bring in talent with particular expertise from outside the company. The risk in bringing in new people to the organization is well understood and in many ways relates to how well they can be assimilated into the corporate culture. If a person with new and valuable know-how can be readily assimilated and their knowledge shared with colleagues then that's good. If the new employee finds it difficult to assimilate for whatever reason colleagues may discount their knowledge no matter how valuable it is. We shall be talking more about corporate culture and knowledge sharing later in this book.

```
┌─ KM Concept#26 ──────────────────────────────────────┐
│                                                       │
│        Understand How Knowledge is Generated          │
│                                                       │
└───────────────────────────────────────────────────────┘
```

Sometimes in order for a company to survive it is essential to bring in new people. This is usually a new CEO who brings with them not only knowledge which may transform an ailing enterprise but a new set of values which the organization needs to adopt in order for survival. Such persons usually have the power to remove employees who are blockages to the procedures, shared values and so forth. Employees in possession of valuable knowledge who are trying to assimilate into a new organization need to understand the rules of the organization if they are to ensure that their message does not fall on to barren ground.

3 As a Product of a Mentoring Programme

Mentoring programmes have been around for thousands of years. In the golden age of Greece young men frequently had mentors who would introduce them to mathematical and philosophical concepts, and teach

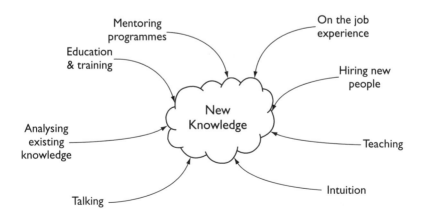

Figure 7.1 Generation of new knowledge

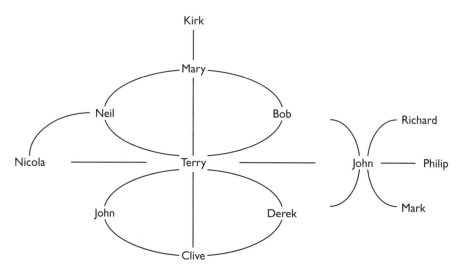

Figure 7.2 Knowledge flows

them the art of debate. Mentoring is not the same as training apprentices as it has more to do with the development of the individual. Mentoring programmes are now popular in many western corporations where an individual may have a small group of employees for whom he or she provides a mentoring role which might include advice on education, developing job related knowledge and so forth, in order to advance their competence and proficiency. The focus is on the individuals and their personal development both in terms of managerial experience and the inner self. Each person is a unique situation, and in order to aide each individual to be his or her absolute best, mentors need to respond to individual needs. Mentors may take on a teaching role from time to time, but in general they are guides who help each individual locate and travel his or her own path.

4 As a Product of Certain Types of Education and Training

We have already spoken about the relationship between competence, proficiency and how education plays a key role in the development of new competencies. However it is worth noting again that a very well educated person is not necessarily a very knowledgeable one where the required job related knowledge calls for a high degree of proficiency. That added value only comes with on the job training and experience. The world we live in today moves so fast that it is impossible to imagine that employees go to college in their early twenties and that's the last time they experience formal training. In some areas of expertise such as semiconductor design, and the application of the Internet to business, it has been estimated that the knowledge possessed by a graduate upon leaving college is out of date in less than nine months. There are two attitudes individuals can take in response to this situation: either sit back and assume that if the organization needs some new know-how then employees will be sent on a course; or alternatively individuals can take responsibility for their own life and education, and become their own driving force to keep moving forward, planning their own education and training. The latter approach is recommended. The distressing side effect of this situation is that as a society we are splitting in two. The educated and the uneducated. Sadly the uneducated in our current society are discovering that it is increasingly difficult to remain permanently employed.

5 By Generating New Knowledge Through Analysis

Generating knowledge through analysis refers to the situation where new knowledge is grown as a result of assimilating, learning and ultimately improving upon existing knowledge. Thus new knowledge is created. The value of this process is proven by the very high number of patents which are registered which represent an improvement on an existing patent, rather than a completely new invention. Generation of new knowledge through analysis is used in organizations at all levels from meetings to discuss why something went wrong to scientific analysis of experiments which may take years. Sometimes it's hard to learn from analysis if the object of analysis is related to the individual who is doing the analysing. In that case it's sometimes useful to use outside agents such as consultants. Sadly they are frequently criticized for telling us things we think we already know, but somehow haven't quite been able to recognize as knowledge we already have.

┌─ KM Concept#27 ────────────────────────────────────┐
│   │
│   Knowledge is Fluid – Know How it Flows   │
│   │
└──┘

6 THROUGH INTERACTION WITH OUTSIDE AGENTS

Stimulation provided by outside agents is invaluable in bringing new knowledge into the organization. Forms of strategic relationship such as joint sales, marketing or even outsourcing teach us lessons about manufacturing, sales and marketing of our own products and services which we would fail to see by ourselves. Indeed it is difficult sometimes to see the wood for the trees. Other invaluable outside agents are academic institutions and consulting houses. In general the link between academia and industry is not strong enough for either party to truly benefit from the potentially rich relationship, and small companies think they have to be prepared to sponsor research projects to the tune of hundreds of thousands of dollars before academics will be interested in their work. This is an avenue that all corporations should investigate thoroughly on a regular basis. The advantage to the academic institution is enormous too. How can they possibly prepare to help corporations grow employees if they are isolated from the ever changing business environment?

7 THROUGH BRAINSTORMING

Brainstorming is a great way of trying to move the corporate head forward and generate new knowledge. However brainstorming sessions can be dominated by a few outspoken individuals who may inadvertently prevent other group members from participating. The way to prevent this is to manage the brainstorm. Edward de Bono's 'Six Thinking Hats' is a great method to use in a brainstorming session and one which we have used successfully on many occasions. The basic idea is to 'unscramble thinking so that a thinker is able to use one thinking mode at a time – instead of trying to do everything at once'. The six thinking hats are each represented by a colour:

- white hat: virgin white, pure facts, figures and information;
- red hat: seeing red, emotions and feelings, also hunch and intuition;

- black hat: devil's advocate, negative judgement, why it will not work;
- yellow hat: sunshine, brightness and optimism, positive, constructive, opportunity;
- green hat: fertile, creative, plants sprinkling from seeds, movement, provocation;
- blue hat: cool and control, orchestra conductor, think about thinking.

During a brainstorming session participants must all wear the same 'colour hat' until ideas run dry, then you move on to the next colour, depending upon what type of thinking is required next. De Bono explains the six thinking hats method in detail in his book of the same name.

8 BY TALKING!

Discussions with colleagues generate new knowledge through interactions and sparking off each other's ideas. It's incorrect to think that such discussions need be formal; quite the contrary. Informal walking around, standing by the espresso machine, or in the smoking room can form the life blood of knowledge generation and dissemination in company. I recall one English engineer who was working in collaboration with a Silicon Valley company who for some months failed to realize that the reason he did not know what was going on in his project was that he didn't drink Coke, and thus never hung out around the Coke machine. His team mates did of course drink Coke; lots of it – and therefore spent lots of time around the Coke machine buying and drinking it. After a period of time he noticed that there frequently seemed to be a bunch of his colleagues in this particular place so he hung out there to, and therefore discovered how in that particular culture they shared and discussed knowledge they were discovering about the project they worked on.

9 BY TEACHING

Teaching is a wonderful way of learning. When I taught at college every year I would volunteer to teach something I knew very little about. True, preparation for these courses was onerous, but my students always said they were among my better lectures, and I can't count the number of times

I have had revelations about the subject matter as I was speaking in a lecture theatre. The stress and rigour of teaching forces us to think in a more structured way in order to explain ourselves. The pressure of two hundred eyes (many in much smarter heads) staring at you makes you try that much harder, and then insight occurs.

10 BY LISTENING TO YOUR INTUITION

Intuition is knowing without knowing why you know. We work in an environment that has taught us only to believe what we can see and touch. The human potential is much greater than its ability to think about and function in a physical world, after all we are each composed of mind, body and spirit. All of us have had experiences where we quickly think we 'know' whether a deal is good or bad, a person is trustworthy or not, or whether a certain approach to solve a problem will work or not. Because we can't explain that to others, and even ourselves, we discard it, replacing it with some supposed truth we have learnt in the past. 'If he worked for such and such a company he must be a good salesman', 'the deal on paper looks good, I can't find anything wrong with it'. Yet in the back of our minds we know this individual is a rotten salesperson, and the deal is a bad one, yet we ignore our little voice, hire the person and sign up for the deal. How often have you done that? How often was it a mistake?

Several years ago we were doing diligence on a deal for a client. The deal was complex and throughout the meeting I just knew it was no good. Our client was being asked to invest a large amount of money in this venture. Unable to pin down exactly why I thought the whole thing was a pretence I did something I have never done before: I called Scotland Yard and asked if the names of the key individuals were known to the police in relation to any questionable business dealings, explaining the situation I was in. An officer called me back in less than 10 minutes to tell me that none of the individuals were known to the police but then said, 'Look just because we don't know about them doesn't mean they are trustworthy. If you are experienced in looking at deals for investors, and you think there is something wrong with the deal, there probably is, go with your intuition.' I was shocked. Some months later I discovered that the Fraud Squad had been called in to investigate the business venture.

Figure 7.3 Use your intuition

Our minds have access to a great deal of knowledge most of us can't tap into at will. Indeed that would be an extremely nice skill to have. But it's worth trying to open up that door to see what intuition can tell us, and how we can use it to further our knowledge and awareness.

CROSSING BOUNDARIES

In all of the methods outlined above it is also worth considering the value of inter-disciplinary interaction in the workplace. Software engineers can learn a lot from interacting with customers by spending a couple of weeks on the customer support line. After all there is no better way of understanding how easy the product is to use than to have to talk to people all day who are having a problem using it. Product teams can learn a lot from looking at product development from the perspective of marketing or manufacturing. I wonder how many products have been designed by engineers, built and then shipped to customers only to discover that the thing can't be maintained in the field, or when it breaks down it's too costly to repair. Such mistakes can be avoided by having an inter-disciplinary team involved in the design of the product. Knowledge learnt in this way is carried on throughout the life of the engineer and he now knows to look at aspects of manufacturability because of that experience.

Sinks, Sources and Gatekeepers

Do you know who are the creatives in your organization? Who were the people responsible for solving major problems? Yes? No? Why not? Consider a small organization of say ten people. Somewhere near the top of the organization there will probably be a person who has more knowledge to solve problems and be creative than the rest of the group. In a ten person company there may be two people, probably both would have a fair amount of power and prestige in the company because the company is so small. How their expertise is used in the company will probably be fairly obvious. They will work on difficult assignments, handle important clients and so forth. Their activity is very public and observable. These people may be the originators of knowledge within the company. They will define procedures, design and implement methodologies and so forth. In a ten person company disseminating this type of expertise is not too difficult as small teams can be put together to learn on the job.

KM Concept#28

Know Who are the Sources and Sinks of Knowledge

Now consider a fifty person company. Let's assume that the statistics are fairly consistent, so in a fifty person company there may be ten to fifteen people who are the best problem solvers, creatives and so forth. Do you know who they are in the organization? Are there more than fifteen of them? How is their knowledge transferred from one person to another? When we consider these types of individuals in a company we need to consider several issues:

Where does knowledge originate within the organization?
Where does knowledge flow within the organization?
How does knowledge flow within the organization?
Where are the sources and sinks of knowledge in the organization?
What mechanisms are used to facilitate the dissemination of knowledge in the organization?

Where Does Knowledge Originate within the Organization?

Looking to see where various types of knowledge originate within the organization means identifying sources of knowledge. The sources may vary wildly in terms of the way they add value to the company. Value may be added due to knowledge about a customer account, how to perform maintenance, how to prepare a particular type of document and so forth. Of course everyone thinks up something useful from time to time – that's why it's best to consider how solutions to critical problems are solved. Originators of knowledge within the organization are known as sources. Any manager worth their salt should know who in their organization is a source. That's easy to do when the organization is small but when it's large, or requires inter-disciplinary skills it can be difficult unless you have a methodology and mechanism for tracking knowledge flows.

Where does Knowledge Flow within the Organization?

Assuming that there are individuals in the organization who generate new knowledge of whatever variety it is then important to know where that knowledge flows within the organization. Ideally it should flow towards people who can be empowered by it to better respond to customers' needs or to fix a problem more efficiently. This is our goal, to have all pertinent knowledge in the right place at the right time, and with someone proficient to use it when necessary. So if this is not happening in your organization it means that for some reason it is getting blocked in its flow. Where this happens a sink is identified. So understanding where sources and sinks are located helps us to understand where knowledge is flowing.

Wanna Be King For a Day?

How long will those who keep knowledge to themselves be king? Not for long. Proponents of the mushroom management principle don't have much power when knowledge changes as rapidly as it does today. At best you can be king for a day, then the focus moves on somewhere else.

Unlike the old days when bad managers could survive for an entire career hoarding knowledge and using it as the basis for their power, today such individuals are found out quickly and maybe next time are isolated from the flow of knowledge in the organization. Sometimes the sink is appropriate as where the knowledge has stopped flowing is appropriate because of its nature. Sometimes it is totally inappropriate for knowledge to 'get stuck' somewhere, and the individual who is hanging on to it is someone who believes that knowledge is power. Such individuals are dinosaurs in third millennium companies.

Being in the Know

From time to time in an organization there is a person who seems to have no direct responsibility for anything yet they are indispensable. They don't seem to do anything but talk to people. They are in the corridor, in

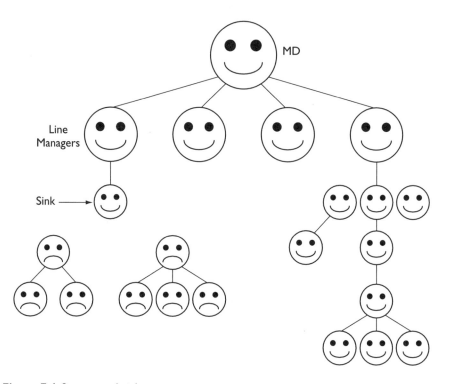

Figure 7.4 Sources and sinks

the cafeteria, by the coffee machine, in their office, on the phone and in the smoking room. Such persons can easily be re-engineered out of the company as it looks like they add no value. Maybe they do? Most organizations have someone who just seems to know how to get things done, or who would know how to solve a particular problem, or who remembers that the company did a survey in that geography in the early 1980s. These are the gatekeepers, and they are very important individuals who provide the lubricant for knowledge to flow around the organization. Fire these people and links to the past are permanently severed. So gatekeepers act as conduits for knowledge to flow around the organization when it runs out of momentum.

Knowing where sinks, sources and gatekeepers are tells us quite a lot about how the organization is working and to some extent how healthy it is with respect to sharing knowledge.

How Does Knowledge Flow Within the Organization?

So if knowledge flows from sources to sinks how does it get there? There are several ways this happens in an organization:

1 through informal networks;
2 through formal networks;
3 through briefing and debriefing;
4 through documents;
5 through workshops;
6 through shared experience encounters.

1 Through Informal Networks

Informal networks within the organization include the not-so casual conversations concerning business which occur in the cafeteria, pub or bar, around the Coke machine and in the smoking room. One CEO who had banned smoking in his company, yet still smokes cigarettes himself outside with other employees told me that not only was it the best way to find out what was happening in his company, but in the British winter it was also the fastest way!

2 Through Formal Networks

Formal networks are those which are organized around a particular subject area such as a quality network, or a knowledge management network. These individuals are bonded together by a common interest in knowledge of a particular nature.

┌─ KM Concept#29 ────────────────────────────┐
│   │
│   Know the Whereabouts of Knowledge Networks │
│   │
└──┘

3 Through Briefing and Debriefing

Briefing prior to an assignment and then debriefing upon its conclusion are two excellent ways of both uncovering knowledge that has been generated and disseminating it through the group. This method has long been used by the military to ensure teamwork at the beginning of an assignment, then make sure maximum intelligence is gathered from the group at the end of the exercise. The issue then of course is how to disseminate that information to others in the organization.

4 Through Documents

Documents have always been a classical method of recording data, information and knowledge about a particular issue. I cringe to think how much time has been spent on the creation of documents versus the impact they have had on an organization. One problem in creating documents as a repository for knowledge is finding some way of indexing them to ensure that their content is self-explanatory. If you know you need a document on a particular subject it's usually easy to locate it, but if you aren't aware that you need to read a particular document it doesn't exist for you. Thus you are isolated from that knowledge.

5 Through Workshops

Workshops are a good method for disseminating knowledge within the organization and it's a good idea to cultivate a culture where employees share experiences and knowledge gained from particular projects. Workshops need not be high profile, and indeed can usefully form part of a regular lunchtime programme. Disseminating knowledge about how particular situations have been dealt with, how customer problems have been solved enables others to adopt similar practices. By planning a variety of workshops to include technical, marketing, sales, administration and manufacturing which the majority of the company can attend not only helps employees understand the workings of the company better, they also gain a clearer understanding of the role they play within the company, and feel involved.

6 Through Shared Experience Encounters

In recent years there has been a growing trend towards activities which cause groups within the company to bond. Adventure weekends, off road driving competitions and more recently team scuba diving events truly mean that the cost of not working as a team can cause serious injury to colleagues. Whilst not all these activities need to be life threatening, knowledge about colleagues and how they behave in a particular situation is shared on such experiences and it's definitely worthwhile planning these into a corporate programme which includes knowledge management.

WHAT MECHANISMS ARE USED TO FACILITATE THE DISSEMINATION OF KNOWLEDGE IN THE ORGANIZATION?

The advent of the Internet and groupware products such as Lotus Notes have opened up new opportunities for sharing knowledge. However we do not concentrate on the details of these products in this book as there is a tendency to assume that implementing software such as Lotus Notes means that you have implemented your knowledge sharing programme in the company. You haven't. You are Lotus Notes users. Computer systems always have been, and always will be the railway track upon which a solution can be deployed. Knowledge management solutions are just the same, and although there are no product based solutions (yet), which have been specifically designed to provide an infrastructure for knowledge management, there will be in the near future.

That's not to say that groupware is not useful. It is. As a mechanism for recording experiences in a work environment they are very effective. But as we have already discussed, knowledge is not just knowledge which can be written down in a document – it also comprises a wealth of knowledge that cannot be codified, and an effective knowledge management mechanism will provide facilities to access a wide variety of knowledge within the organization.

8

Corporate Culture and Knowledge Management

This is a really key issue. And in order to understand the impact of corporate culture we need to talk a bit about exactly what corporate culture is. Simply defined, corporate culture is 'The Way We Do Things Around Here'. Corporate culture is invisible and formidable, as those of us who have ever clashed with it understand only too well. The culture of the company provides the context within which business is done. It embraces the values of the business which in turn will determine how employees feel about deadlines, quality, unhappy customers and so on.

So how do you know what the culture of a company is if you can't see it? Well there are a number of key indicators which give us insight into the way an organization works. Below we will look at various aspects of

---

> **'The way we do things around here'**
>
> - A widely shared philosophy
> - A business culture
> - Rituals and ceremonies
> - Champions and heroes
> - The context for all our business activities

---

corporate culture, some of which you might recognize in your own company. Such indicators include:

1 rituals;
2 ceremonies;
3 measures of success;
4 corporate beliefs;
5 values.

1 RITUALS

Rituals are the events which take place in the company and serve to provide some sort of bonding. They may be company picnics, bagel mornings, ghastly gift events, corporate sports days, beer busts and so on. Mostly they bring employees together in some informal way to share an experience which may be serious or just for fun. Participation in ritual is desirable if the individual wants to remain in the 'flow'. These events are theoretically optional, that is the individual does not have to attend, but non-attendance sends out a message to colleagues saying, 'I am not one of the pack'.

> **Rituals and ceremonies**
>
> - The beer bust
> - The winners circle
> - The Christmas party
> - Employee of the month
> - The birthday cake
> - Bagel day
> - Dress for success
> - The annual plum fight and sports day
> - The staff meetings

Rituals and ceremonies (cont.)

- The wedding ceremony
- The doughnuts on Tuesday mornings
- Secretaries day
- April Fools Day
- Jeans day

Mad Dogs and Englishmen

Several years ago I left England and went to work at Sun Microsystems in California as a product marketing manager. This was in the mid-1980s and as yet Sun had not gone public. I recall being told that the company would be holding a picnic and I was asked if I was going. As a British person the concept of a company picnic was totally bizarre, but I went along anyway. During the afternoon we gathered around a ducking machine, where the victim was to sit on a seat over a large water container some eight feet deep. Employees were then invited to throw a ball at a target, and if they hit the target the victim's seat would collapse, plunging them into the barrel of water below. So far so good, but to my amazement Scott McNealy, our CEO, climbed up on to the chair in shorts and a T-shirt, and was duly plunged into the barrel of water to the delight of the assembled audience. Now, from my perspective seeing the CEO in shorts was enough of a culture shock (fortunately British male CEO's don't typically display their knees), but in those days to plunge a British CEO into a barrel of water was unthinkable. I couldn't speak. But then the entire executive team followed suit, and all finished up wet. This is apparently perfectly acceptable in California. After several months at Sun I woke up one morning with the realization that although the Americans and the British speak the same language (well nearly), and I thought I had understood what was going on, in reality I didn't have a clue. This indicated a lack of understanding about the deeper values and beliefs not only of a company, but of a country as well. I still cringe at the memory of the occasion when Scott came up to me in the cafeteria in front of a large crowd. I had done something useful with a particular customer account, so he said 'Well done, gimme five', and I replied 'Five what?'.

KM Concept#30

Corporate Culture Must Support Knowledge Sharing

2 CEREMONIES

Corporate ceremonies are more formal occasions where individuals or groups of individuals are usually recognized in some way. Examples include employee of the month, salesperson of the year, Winners Circle and so forth. The honouring of certain individuals is a reflection of the values of the company. If the company places a high value on customer service then individuals who reflect that value are recognized and appropriately honoured. This reinforces the value system, and demonstrates that the company is not just paying lip service to it.

3 MEASURES OF SUCCESS

Methods of measuring success are an interesting area of discussion and also a reflection of the corporate value system. What is success? On one occasion a collaboration was launched between a British and an American company on a semiconductor project and the British team sent three engineers over to Silicon Valley. The collaboration was led by the US team, with the British writing the software. The project dropped behind schedule, and unfortunately the two teams were not communicating very well. The US team leader decided to modify and reduce the functionality of the device in order to hit the deadline. By the time the UK team realized this, vast amounts of code had been written for the wrong piece of hardware. The code had to be hugely modified. The British simply couldn't believe that the US engineer had the power to modify the original specification, nor that the deadline was more important than completing the project as specified. The collaboration dissolved. What was at the root of the problem was the fact that the cultures of the two companies were very different. In the US company hitting deadlines was of utmost importance. For the UK company engineering excellence was more important. Now that's not to say that the US company produced shabby engineering; they didn't. It's just that the measures of success were different.

4 CORPORATE BELIEFS

Corporate beliefs are beliefs about the company that bond employees. Examples include 'At Avis we try harder', 'Rolls Royce make the finest car in the world', the old Apple catch phrase 'One home one computer' and so on. Beliefs serve to reinforce corporate goals and are another window on what you can expect to find happening in a particular corporate culture.

5 VALUES

Values are the baseline for employee behaviour in a company. These range widely in nature from how employees treat each other and in turn are treated; how the company responds to customer problems and treats its customers. Whether or not a consulting company uses 'associates' or only its own consultants and so forth. Values are usually pretty much black and white: either we do not do that here or we do.

CULTURE CHARACTERIZATIONS

Hero Based Culture

There are many ways of characterizing corporate cultures, but it seems to me that there are a few which keep popping up over and over again. The first is the hero based culture. Hero based cultures are those which value individuals who pull off heroic feats. I recall one company where a software guru was rumoured to have rewritten part of the operating system for a computer on an aeroplane trip from the USA to the UK – and the code ran first time. Another story concerns a salesperson who managed to achieve double his sales quota in a particular year and yet another where a salesperson was so confident that he could achieve his target that he approached the VP of sales with a proposition that he not be paid a salary – but instead receive a higher percentage on every sale he made. A final story tells of a project where the gap between the blueprint the design engineers had produced and what the manufacturing engineers needed to build a new workstation was too huge to bridge. So one of the design team was asked to singlehandedly build the machine by hand by a certain date.

If he could do it he would receive a new Porsche. He did, and he got the car. These people are heroes. They perform superhuman tasks and in return they receive the adulation of their peers, and hopefully they are remunerated accordingly. They act as role models in the company. Hero based cultures sometimes comprise small teams of say five to ten people. The team is small enough that when the task is complete everyone can be recognized as a hero. This differs from organizations where the individual is not the one who is recognized, but either the boss or the department, or a group. I recall talking with one UK engineer about how excellence was recognized in his company and he told me that the best accolade was to have 'Distinguished Engineer' printed on one's business card. When I began to talk about the hero based cultures I had worked in over the years he remarked, 'Yuk, how vulgar!' – it takes all kinds I guess.

— KM Concept#31 —

Corporate Heroes Share Knowledge

Family Based Cultures

Family based cultures are those which look after the group as a whole. Hewlett Packard is often cited as an example of a family based culture. This may be borne out by HP's behaviour in the past in difficult economic times. When other companies were making employees redundant HP cut the working week in an effort not to make employees redundant; when salary cuts were necessary, HP cut the salary of higher paid employees rather than the lower paid. This type of behaviour reinforces values that were instilled in the company by its founders decades ago.

Entrepreneurial Cultures

This type of culture is one where each employee is encouraged to think about the company as if it were their own company. There is a general belief that the responsibility for sales, happy customers and so forth is the responsibility of all employees not just those who happen to have a job title with sales or customer support in it. In this type of company each employee is encouraged to look for business opportunities the company can pursue all the time. Consulting companies and legal partnerships are sometimes like this.

EMPOWER, ENABLE, ENERGIZE

By now some of you may be thinking, 'That's fine for some companies but ours would never behave in any of these ways'. That may well be the case if employees within the organization are not empowered. From time to time we come across a company whose CEO will say, 'all our employees are empowered', then when you look down the hierarchy you find that in some places managers are encouraging employees to be empowered and in other places they have no intention at all of permitting empowerment. The important thing to note about power is that it can't be given. It must be taken. So the people at the top of the company can talk about empowerment until the end of time, but if individual employees are not permitted to take and utilize power they will never become empowered. One client of ours in the software business decided that if they were going to survive a successful transition into the third millennium they had to be able to design, mount and complete a wide variety of business collaborations. They asked us to design a two day residential course to support that goal and over a two year period some 80 middle managers attended the course with the specific goal of learning how to design, mount and measure business collaborations. At the end of the two year period we deduced that it had been nothing but an interesting educational experiment. The culture of the company would not enable empowerment for employees to do anything. True, there were a few hot spots in the company where managers really encouraged employees to go for it, but in general the training course didn't change the way the company worked. We have seen this happen over and over in large companies, especially those which are geographically distributed and divisionalized, in which cases divisions or geographic units have developed their own culture.

What is happening here is that the management philosophy is at odds with the corporate culture, and a stalemate results. The culture protects the organization from change. That's good sometimes, but bad when there is a real need for culture to change if the organization is to survive. Changing corporate culture takes a long, long time; is painful and expensive. In their book on the subject Deal and Kennedy (1982) estimate the cost to a company to be in excess of 10 per cent of its annual budget for the personnel whose behaviour needs to be changed. If the desired change is radical that process can take years. If the change is drastic it may be cheaper to shut the company down and start all over again.

Bursting the Bubble

From time to time we come across a situation where the employees of a company just seem to have forgotten what they come to work for every day. Sadly it seems that in some organizations procedures have been cast in stone, and no matter how ludicrous the results of sticking to procedure, they never deviate. What follows is an example of an organization which doesn't appear to have collided with the notion of empowerment just yet. The text is taken from Thomas Stewart's book on *Intellectual Capital*, and is purported to be real correspondence between a guest and staff at a London hotel. I prefer to think that this could only happen in England but I doubt it! Many apologies to those of you who have seen this before – I just couldn't resist including it.

Dear Maid,
Please do not leave any more of those little bars of soap in my bathroom since I have brought my own bath-sized Dial. Please remove the six unopened little bars of soap from the shelf under the medicine chest and another there in the shower soap dish. They are in my way.
Thank you
S Berman

Dear Room 635,
I am not your regular maid. She will be back tomorrow, Thursday, from her day off, I took the 3 hotel soaps out of your shower soap dish as you requested. The 6 bars on your shelf I took out of your way and put on top of your Kleenex dispenser in case you would change your mind. This leaves only the 3 bars I left today which my instructions from management is to leave 3 soaps daily. I hope this is satisfactory.
Kathy, Relief Maid

Dear Maid,

I hope you are my regular maid. Apparently Kathy did not tell you about my note to her concerning the little bars of soap. When I got back to my room this evening I found you had added 3 little Camays to the shelf under my medicine cabinet. I am going to be here in the hotel for two weeks and have brought my own bath-size Dial so I won't need those 6 little Camay's which are on the shelf. They are in my way when shaving, brushing teeth etc. Please remove them.

S Berman

Dear Mr Berman,

My day off was last Wed, so the relief maid left 3 hotel soaps which we are instructed by management. I took the 6 soaps which were in your way off the shelf and put them in the soap dish where your Dial was. I put the Dial in the medicine cabinet for your convenience. I didn't remove the 3 complementary soaps which are always placed inside the medicine cabinet for all new check-ins and which you did not object to when you checked in last Monday. Please let me know if I can be of further assistance.

Your regular maid,

Dotty

Dear Mr Berman,

The assistant manager, Mr Kensedder, informed me this A.M. that you called him last evening and said you were unhappy with your maid service. I have assigned a new girl to your room. I hope you will accept my apologies for any past inconvenience. If you have any future complaints please contact me so I can give it my personal attention. Call extension 1108 between 8am and 5pm. Thank you.

Elaine Carmen, Housekeeper

Dear Miss Carmen,

It is impossible to contact you by phone since I leave the hotel for business at 7.45 AM and don't get back before 5.30 or 6 PM. That's the reason I called Mr Kensedder last night. You were already off duty. I only asked Mr Kensedder if he can do anything about those little bars

of soap. The new maid you assigned me must have thought I was a new check-in today, since she left another 3 bars of hotel soap in my medicine cabinet along with her regular delivery of 3 bars on my bathroom shelf. In just 5 days here I have accumulated 24 little bars of soap. Why are you doing this to me?
S Berman

Dear Mr Berman,
Your maid, Kathy, has been instructed to stop delivering soap to your room and remove the extra soaps. If I can be of further assistance, please call extension 1108 between 8AM and 5PM. Thank you,
Elaine Carmen, Housekeeper

Dear Mr Kensedder,
My bath-size Dial is missing. Every bar of soap was taken from my room including my own bath-size Dial. I came in late last night and had to call the bellhop to bring me 4 little Cashmere Bouquets.
S Berman

Dear Mr Berman,
I have informed our housekeeper, Elaine Carmen, of your soap problem. I cannot understand why there was no soap in your room since our maids are instructed to leave 3 bars of soap each time they service a room. The situation will be rectified immediately. Please accept my apologies for the inconvenience.
Martin L. Kensedder, Assistance Manager

Dear Miss Carmen,
Who the hell left 54 little bars of Camay in my room? I came in last night and found 54 little bars of soap. I don't want 54 little bars of Camay. I want my one damn bar of bath-size Dial. Do you realize I have 54 bars of soap in here? All I want is my bath-size Dial. Please give me back my bath-size Dial.
S Berman

Dear Mr Berman,

You complained of too much soap in your room so I had them removed. Then you complained to Mr Kensedder that all your soap was missing so I personally returned them. The 24 Camays which had been taken and the 3 Camays you are supposed to receive daily. I don't know anything about the 4 Cashmere Bouquets. Obviously your maid, Kathy, did not know I had returned your soaps so she also brought 24 Camays plus the 3 daily Camays. I don't know where you got the idea that this hotel issues bath-size Dial. I was able to locate some bath-size Ivory which I left in your room.

Elaine Carmen,

Housekeeper

Dear Miss Carmen,

Just a short note to bring you up to date on my latest soap inventory. As of today I possess:

On shelf under medicine cabinet – 18 Camay in 4 stacks of 4 and 1 stack of 2.

On Kleenex dispenser – 11 Camay in 2 stacks of 4 and 1 stack of 3.

On bedroom dresser – 1 stack of 3 Cashmere Bouquet, 1 stack of 4 hotel-size Ivory, and 8 Camay in 2 stacks of 4.

Inside medicine cabinet – 14 Camay in 3 stacks of 4 and 1 stack of 2.

In shower soap dish – 6 Camay, very moist.

On northeast corner of tub – 1 Cashmere Bouquet slightly used.

On northwest corner of tub – 6 Camays in 2 stacks of 3.

Please ask Kathy when she services my room to make sure the stacks are neatly piled and dusted. Also, please advise her that stacks of more than 4 have a tendency to tip. May I suggest that my bedroom window sill is still not in use and will make an excellent spot for future soap deliveries. One more item, I have purchased another bar of bath-sized Dial which I am keeping in the hotel vault in order to avoid further misunderstandings.

S Berman

KM Concept#32

All Employees Have Knowledge About Corporate Goals

LOOKING AT CORPORATE CULTURES

When looking at a company there are some indicators that might tell you something about the culture of the company. The reason that this is of interest is that the culture of the company will be either a hindrance or help if a knowledge management programme is to be introduced. So in addition to trying to determine whether the culture is hero based, family based, etc. it is worth looking at some other indicators. Mostly we are looking for indicators of openness and an awareness to share.

Culture Indicators

- What do Company X people wear?
- What kind of jokes do Company X people tell?
- What do Company X people think about families?
- What do Company X people think about company Y?
- How do Company X people relate to their bosses?
- How do Company X people hire and fire?
- How are Company X people rewarded for doing a good job?
- What kind of guy is a good Company X employee?
- What do Company X people think about collaborative ventures? . . . Why?
- What hours do people work?

Who's for Knowledge Management?

Deploying a knowledge management programme in a company means establishing a culture together with systems to ensure that the huge variety of knowledge which exists in a company can be shared with the employees who need to use it at any time and anywhere. That's a pretty tall order. The difficulty comes not so much from a systems perspective, as we already have computer systems that can respond to around the clock, around the planet demands. The difficult part in knowledge management systems from a cultural perspective is getting people to believe that sharing knowledge will be beneficial not only to the company but also to themselves.

Some companies already have sharing as part of their culture. Companies with active empowered employees are already sharing power, responsibility and accountability. Companies that share equity with employees are sharing the benefits of successful business with employees.

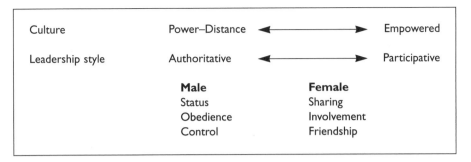

Figure 8.1 Knowledge management and corporate culture

Companies that share profits with employees are distributing financial rewards when the company is profitable. Other companies are not sharers. Founders keep all the equity or split it between family members instead of employees. Profits are only paid out to shareholders, not to employees who are not equity holders. Managers won't let employees make even the most trivial decisions, even worse, they avoid responsibility themselves by having a hierarchical system of authorization which ensures that the CEO is responsible for every single decision which is made in the company. Legally the CEO is always responsible, but hopefully he or she hires and rewards proficient staff who ought to be able to be held accountable.

When we think about the nature of companies that might be sharers it's useful to have a scale which I call the male–female spectrum. This has nothing to do with sex. The terms are used to characterize two types of companies: power–distance and empowered (Figure 8.1).

Power–Distance Cultures

Power–distance cultures are those where there is power and distance between the higher and lower members of the organization. This type of culture is characterized as masculine, and attributes would typically include management via hierarchy and supervision. It is a very controlled culture. Individuals would not be encouraged to be entrepreneurial, innovative or step out of line. It is interesting to speculate in power–distance cultures what would motivate the individual to share knowledge with any of his or her colleagues. If the overriding cultural norm is that those with power keep subordinates at a distance, then where knowledge *is* power it would be normal for the individual to keep it to him- or herself in order to keep that power. So it follows that in such cultures a new method of motivation needs to be found to encourage individuals to share knowledge. Many workers in the knowledge management field have suggested that the way around this is to financially remunerate employees for sharing knowledge. Apart from the fact that logistically this would be extremely difficult to measure and manage, it would be encouraging individuals to break with the cultural norm for the company and take a position against it. This typically leads to the expulsion of the individual by the masses who embrace the culture. The only way around this problem is to change the behaviour of all employees, so the majority do not reject the minority. If that is achieved the culture will have moved towards an empowered culture, as sharing will be embodied in the resulting culture. The problem with culture is that one of its roles is to protect the company from change. We have already spoken about the potential cost of such an action, more than 10 per cent of the budget for every employee needing to change his or her behaviour, per annum.

So for power–distance cultures the prognosis for adopting knowledge management is not particularly good.

Empowered Cultures

Cultures where employees are empowered tend to be more female, with individuals sharing power, responsibility, decision making and so on. Where there already is a culture of sharing, introducing a knowledge sharing philosophy has a greater chance of success than it would in organizations which typically don't share anything.

The Exception that Proves the Rule

The distinction between these two types of cultures is by no means distinct. Take for example a large engineering organization where the management chain is power–distance through and through. Nothing can be done unless the appropriate signatures are on the sheet right up to the Directors of the company. In this type of organization you would have thought that there would be huge resistance to the introduction of anything which upset the power–distance regime. Me too, but I was wrong. When we deployed a pilot knowledge management system in such an organization we discovered that when it came to technical knowledge, expertise and know-how, engineers were extremely pleased to share the knowledge they possessed on any subject with any person in the organization. This reflected the aspect of engineering excellence which was also embodied in the organization and co-habited with the power–distance culture. From an engineering perspective it was desirable to have the best possible knowledge about possible solutions to problems, and to know where in the organization the key talent existed. So the lesson to be learnt here is not to be too hasty in coming to a cursory conclusion concerning corporate culture. Look at exactly why knowledge needs to be shared in the organization, and the attitude of the individuals who will be both sharing and benefiting from its sharing.

9

Establishing an Infrastructure for Knowledge Management

If a knowledge management system is to be implemented there are a number of infrastructure issues to consider before attempting to launch a system. Let's start by recalling what corporate infrastructure is. Infrastructure assets are a wide range of assets which include management philosophy, corporate culture, management and business processes, financial relations, methodologies and IT systems. Examples include methodologies for assessing risk, methods of managing a sales force, financial structure, databases of information on the market or customers, communication systems such as e-mail and teleconferencing systems. Basically, the elements which make up the way the organization works.

The first thing to consider is the relationship between management philosophy, corporate culture and management processes. You will remember that these are important because management philosophy and corporate culture need to be synergistic, that is they must not fight each other. The management processes are those processes that enable the management philosophy to be implemented in the context of the corporate culture. So a knowledge sharing programme:

1 should not be at odds with the management philosophy;
2 should not be at odds with the corporate culture;
3 can have management and business processes implemented which ensure that it is successful.

The last point is very important as it is not worth implementing a knowledge management programme unless it:

1 is embraced by all that use it;
2 can be sustained over a very long period of time;
3 can be measured and monitored in order to ensure it is delivering return on investment;
4 can be grown as an extremely valuable corporate asset.

Let's examine each of these points in turn.

KNOWLEDGE MANAGEMENT NEEDS TO BE EMBRACED BY ALL THAT USE IT

Deploying a knowledge management system in the company is an all or nothing event. To have half the people who ought to be using it not using it defeats its purpose. In that respect it's like e-mail. If the normal way to communicate in a company is e-mail, there is an expectation that everyone reads their e-mail. If particular individuals do not then they are putting themselves at odds with the corporate culture. If the norm is to use a knowledge management system as a corporate resource to look for people with expertise, locate documents, locate methods and so forth and some people do not refer to the system before embarking on projects, they risk making the very mistakes the system was designed to prevent them from making. They are effectively reinventing the wheel, by not using the most appropriate talent for a particular job and so on. Thus if the culture of the organization is to defer to the knowledge management system, by not doing so the individual is at odds with the system. In order for knowledge management to be successful within the organization it has to be 'The way we do things around here'.

KM Concept#33

Knowledge Sharing is the Way We Do Things Around Here

KNOWLEDGE MANAGEMENT SYSTEMS MUST HAVE A LONG LIFE

You have no doubt already gathered that the amount of knowledge which can potentially be contained in a knowledge management programme is huge. Over a period of time it will represent a substantial investment on the part of the company and its employees. One thing is for sure, once data collection has been done, and systems are in place to regularly update the knowledge base, the effort to redevelop or redesign the system will be so huge no one will want to consider doing it. With this type of system you have to get it right first time. We estimate that the minimum length a system should be planned for is twenty years.

KNOWLEDGE MANAGEMENT MUST BE MEASURED AND MONITORED

Remember the old saying about computers – GIGO, garbage in garbage out? The same applies here. If the data, information and knowledge which are put in to the system are not accurate and complete the system will be sub-optimal. So quality measures need to be established to ensure that employees are not only using the system, but that they are updating their records on a regular basis with quality input. This process is fairly easy to set up and enormously rewarding. Managers can tap in to the system on a weekly or monthly basis and look at the records of their reports and of their colleagues. If someone has not modified their records for a month it might be worth finding out what that employee is doing. The amount of time we anticipate that an employee might spend per month updating their record with job related expertise, information on a customer account, lessons learnt and so forth will be about thirty minutes a month. As a CEO I'd love to peruse my corporate memory to look at how things are shaping up, who had figured what out, who had closed business and so forth. This is not intended to be a substitute for actually talking to people, but when the company is large, spread over several sites and involved in multiple projects this facility enables people anywhere in the company to get snapshots of what is actually going on.

THE CORPORATE MEMORY MUST BECOME A VALUABLE CORPORATE ASSET

Unlike human centred assets, the knowledge of the employees, competencies, etc. which belong to the individual, the corporate memory belongs to the company. Therefore it is an asset, and a substantial one which grows in value over time. This is the whole point of the exercise. People change jobs, go on holiday, and eventually die. The corporate memory survives all that and is the property of the company. So by creating a corporate memory we are changing the balance between human centred assets and infrastructure assets.

IT systems provide the railroad tracks upon which knowledge management systems will run. But it should be noted that while the IT system provides the repository for the system and the mechanism for interacting with it, another important part of the system is the users.

SHOULD WE REMUNERATE EMPLOYEES FOR SHARING THEIR KNOWLEDGE?

One of the most frequently asked questions about knowledge management systems is 'How do you know people will use them?'. The most frequent answer I have heard given is that employees should be remunerated financially for sharing rather than hoarding information and knowledge. Personally I just can't see how that can work. In addition it seems to be contrived. After all if a company has a system where all

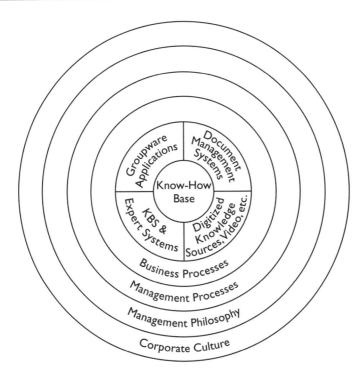

Figure 9.1 The knowledge management system

employees are requested to fill in time sheets we don't pay those who do so more and those who don't less. If weekly reports on customer accounts are required, or security issues need to be adhered to, or job reviews need to be done, they are either done as required or the employee is asked to change their behaviour, disciplined and perhaps eventually fired. It's part of their job to comply. The same is true of a knowledge management system, but more importantly with a knowledge management system it needs to be encompassed as part of 'The way we do things around here', i.e. as part of the culture. So, should we remunerate employees for sharing their knowledge? No.

MANAGEMENT PHILOSOPHY AND KNOWLEDGE SHARING

Management philosophy sets the context for employee attitude to knowledge management in the company, so it goes without saying that the CEO should set the stage by not only participating in a knowledge sharing programme, but also by evangelizing it. The CEO and the executive team should be practising an open style of management, hopefully empowering employees as appropriate. It is interesting to speculate how frequently a CEO's record in the corporate memory would be accessed by employees in the company who want to know what he knows, what his mission is. I'd like to see the CEO record have one of the highest hit rates.

MANAGEMENT PROCESSES

Management processes that reinforce the culture for knowledge management might include the following:

1 job reviews;
2 salary raises;
3 training programmes;
4 mentoring programmes;
5 HR planning.

1 Job Reviews

The record of an employee should reflect a snap-shot picture of the person. The size of the record and its various fields is going to vary from company to company and person to person. However when considering an annual review, many of the important elements which form the basis for the review should be sitting right there in the knowledge management system. In terms of competencies and proficiencies, an individual might have eight competencies for example, four of which they would like to work on in a particular period, for example by taking training courses. Progression can then be shown by way of a polar diagram. It's easy to see whether or not the individual achieved his or her goal. Using the knowledge management system as part of the infrastructure for job reviews not only reinforces use of the system in the company but also sets clear goals for all concerned.

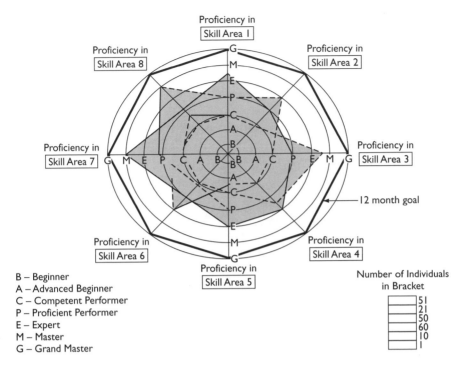

Figure 9.2 Plotting proficiency goals

Legend for the figure:

B – Beginner
A – Advanced Beginner
C – Competent Performer
P – Proficient Performer
E – Expert
M – Master
G – Grand Master

Number of Individuals in Bracket

51
21
50
60
10
1

2 Salary Raises

Confidential information concerning employees, such as salaries, would not typically be a part of the knowledge management system (KMS). That is unless the culture of the company was to have open salary information. In fact it is important to understand that although there is some overlap between the type of information kept in a human resource system and a KMS, the KMS is not intended to replace human resource (HR) systems in any way. In talking to large numbers of HR executives they do perceive that they will be heavy users of the KMS, but not that their own systems and KMS systems will merge.

The basis for salary raises is usually as a function of the job review, and if the KMS is part of the infrastructure used in the job review process, it will have a bearing on salary raises as well. We have been asked whether employees will only update their records just before a salary review, then ignore it for the rest of the year. Computers being the wonderful tools they are, it is very easy to tell whether or not that is happening, and then act accordingly.

3 Training Programmes

In the education section of a person's record there is an option to record not just past training experience but also current and planned training too. By examining the polar diagram of any individual, mentors can determine the best way to help an employee advance from say a journeyman to an expert. First to be competent, then proficient. Plan training first then the development of job related expertise.

4 Mentoring Programmes

Mentoring programmes are designed to assist growth of individual employees in a range of ways, professionally, personally and academically. Mentoring is one of the ways knowledge is transferred from one person to another, so by analysing mentor–mentoree relationships it is possible to get some insight into how knowledge flows in a company. Use of the KMS to track mentoring in a company is another way of reinforcing the use of the KMS. It also provides insight for individuals who perhaps want to develop skills colleagues have already developed. By looking at the record of an individual who has achieved certain proficiencies or competencies it is possible to see how they achieved them.

5 Human Resource Planning

The role of the HR executive is changing rapidly. The job of planning to have the right employees, with the right knowledge, proficiency and so forth in the company is the real challenge HR executives face in the next millennium. This is extremely difficult to do, especially as in many companies the role of the HR executive is sidelined, confused with personnel and not considered to be the central strategic role it really is. In order to perform their function HR executives need a corporate-wide infrastructure which gives them a window on the human resources working in the company. This function is performed by the KMS. Executives we have spoken to about KMS and its potential in the company have stated that such a system would enable them to add significant value to the company, reducing costs simultaneously. Costs associated with recruiting new employees are frequently cited as unnecessary costs as too often the company already has the expertise in place in the company, but the employee may be in the wrong job. There is no infrastructure in companies today which enables HR executives to be aware of the extent of the expertise of every employee.

KM Concept#34

Knowledge Management Supports Human Resource Planning

KMS AND E-MAIL

I can't imagine life without e-mail. E-mail has had a radical impact on companies which use it. Indeed it is the central infrastructure for company and inter-company communication for thousands of companies world-wide. We have changed the way we communicate with each other and our customers and clients as a result of the e-mail revolution. Many of us also run our social lives by e-mail too. This revolution has come about in the last five years, with the widespread adoption of the Internet. E-mail is not new, it has taken nearly two decades for it to become embraced by industry as we now see it. Knowledge management systems will have a similar impact on the company. The central function performed by KMS will add a new dimension to how a company operates. The deeper understanding all employees will have of the potential of the company as a result of access to the KMS will, like e-mail, change the way we grow our employees, put teams together, share knowledge and expertise. Companies that embraced e-mail systems are likely candidates to become early adopters of KMS. I recall as a new employee more than twelve years ago being told that e-mail was the communication infrastructure of Sun Microsystems, and told to make sure I checked it several times a day. Once hooked it's difficult to live without it as the following story (delivered to me by e-mail) demonstrates quite nicely.

The Castaway

A young engineer took a cruise in the Caribbean. It was wonderful. The experience of his life. But it didn't last. A hurricane came and the ship went down almost instantly.

The man found himself swept onto the shore of an isolated island. He looked around. There were some banana and coconut trees, but not much else. So for the next six months he ate bananas, drank coconut juice, and mostly looked to the sea for a ship to come to his rescue.

One day, as he was lying on the beach stroking his beard, he spotted an object in the water. Could it be true, was it a ship? No, from around the corner of the island came a rowboat and in it a gorgeous woman. She was tall, tanned, and her blond hair flowing in the sea breeze gave her an almost ethereal quality. She spotted him too as he was waving and yelling to get her attention, and rowed her boat towards him.

'Where did you come from? How did you get here?' he asked in disbelief.

'I came from the other side of the island,' she said. 'I landed on this island when my cruise ship sank.'

'Amazing,' said he. 'I didn't know anyone else had survived. How many of you are there? Where did you get the rowboat?'

'It is only me. And I made the rowboat myself out of materials I found on the island,' replied the woman.

'But what about tools, how did you do that?'

'It wasn't too difficult,' replied the woman. 'On the southern side of the island there is a very unusual strata of alluvial rock exposed. I found that if I fired it to a certain temperature in my kiln, it melted into forgeable ductile iron. I used that for tools. But enough of that. Where do you live?'

The man confessed that he had been sleeping on the beach.

'Well,' said the woman, 'let's go over to my place.' So they got into the rowboat and left for the other side of the island. There stood her exquisite bungalow, painted blue and white.

'It's not much,' she said, 'but I call it home. Please sit down. Would you like a drink? I have a still, and I can offer you some Pina Colada?' Trying to hide his continued amazement, the man accepted, and they sat down on her couch to talk.

After they had exchanged their stories, the woman asked, 'Tell me, have you always had a beard?'

'No,' replied the man, 'I was clean shaven all my life.'

'Well,' she said, 'if you would like to shave, there is a razor in the bathroom cabinet.' And the man, no longer questioning anything, went up to the bathroom where he found a razor made from a bone handle and two shells honed to a hollow ground edge. He shaved, showered and went back down.

'You look great,' said the woman. 'I think I will go up and slip into something more comfortable myself.' Indeed, after a short while, she returned wearing fig leafs strategically positioned and smelling faintly of gardenia.

'Tell me,' she asked, 'we have both been out here for a very long time with no companionship. You know what I mean. Have you been lonely? Is there anything you really miss? Something all men and woman need? Something that would be really nice to have right now?'

'Yes, there is!' exclaimed the man as he moved closer to the woman, fixing a winsome gaze upon her. 'Tell me . . . Can I check my e-mail?'

┌─ KM Concept#35 ─────────────────────────────────┐
│   │
│   Management Processes Deliver Knowledge Management │
│   │
└───┘

GROWTH OF THE KNOWLEDGE BASED COMPANY

By now some of you may have got the idea that unless you invest in a comprehensive knowledge management infrastructure there is no point in trying. That's not true, there are numerous activities and systems that can be introduced into the company which can have a positive impact on knowledge management. These include:

1 networking and verbal sharing;
2 know-how bases;
3 groupware knowledge sharing;
4 decision support systems;
5 expert and knowledge based systems;
6 intelligent infrastructures.

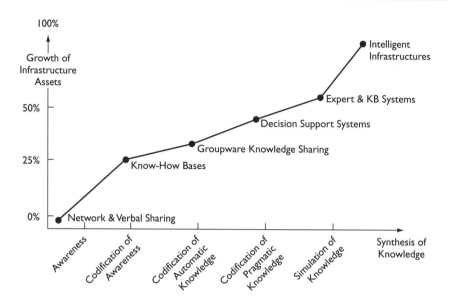

Figure 9.3 Growth of the knowledge based company

1 Networking and Verbal Sharing

Networking and verbal sharing happens in companies already. What we are interested in doing here is promoting networking and knowledge sharing between people on both a formal and informal basis. Ideally networking and verbal sharing of all types of data, information and knowledge are embraced by the corporate culture and nobody really has to think about promoting or evangelizing it. If employees do not exhibit this type of behaviour already then it's worth starting off slowly introducing the idea with key groups working on projects that could benefit from a new approach. In truth if a company is interested in adopting a KMS at some point the employees ought to at least be used to sharing without the aid of systems.

> ┌─ KM Concept#36 ───────────────────────────────
> │
> │   Knowledge Sharing is Part of our Corporate Culture
> │

2 Know-How Bases

The next step is to know what you know. Most companies don't. So start by identifying a group that would benefit from knowing more about their colleagues. The questionnaire in Chapter 10 is a reasonable basis for experimenting, although it all depends on the nature of the organization. Some of our clients have built pilot systems with a group of around twenty people to get a feel for what could be uncovered by such a system. They have been surprised at the breadth and depth of the expertise and knowledge of their own employees. We anticipate that before the year 2000 off-the-shelf products will provide the IT infrastructure for KMS.

3 Groupware Knowledge Sharing

Lotus Notes has led the way with groupware for knowledge sharing. It's not a bad way to start promoting a knowledge sharing philosophy in the company, but at this point Lotus Notes does not offer a comprehensive infrastructure for a KMS as we have discussed it in this book. Organizations we have spoken to that use Lotus Notes seem to be happy with their systems but we feel it is important to note that this is dealing with only one dimension of the knowledge sharing opportunity.

4 Decision Support Systems

Decision support systems have been around for more than twenty years. They are systems which posses knowledge concerning a particular domain, say stock trading, and assist the user to evaluate and make decisions based on an 'expert' perspective. Such systems may be able to process huge quantities of information and data which would be difficult for the individual to do. They provide access to information which is complex to comprehend such as legislation and so on.

5 Expert and Knowledge Based Systems

Expert and knowledge based systems embody knowledge which has typically been gathered from one or more individuals. They function in a limited world, or 'domain', and will perform as an expert based on the data and information given to them. Sometimes they provide an initial opinion or solution based on incomplete data, giving an estimate of the certainty of the conclusion. Expert and knowledge based systems provide deep knowledge in a limited domain, and as such are repositories for knowledge. They provide the infrastructure to manipulate certain types of knowledge, and therefore have a part to play in knowledge management.

6 Intelligent Infrastructures

These systems do not exist as yet. They will be extensions of all of the types of knowledge sharing systems we have discussed. Consider that a system is in place where know-how is captured for every employee. The system is updated regularly by the employees. Perhaps a Lotus Notes application is also running, connected to the know-how base. Management has outlined goals for the organization, and those have in turn formed the basis for an HR strategy with respect to recruiting, staff development and so on. When an individual leaves the organization the system is informed, yet the employee record is not deleted. Such information and knowledge could then be input to a knowledge based system whose function it would be to advise management on the ramifications of changes in the work force. Then the system would advise management of a need to hire new staff, train employees and so forth. The goal of such a system would be to ensure the optimal use of all employee skills to ensure that the company had the right knowledge in the hands of the right person at the right time, all the time.

KM Concept#37

KMS Infrastructures are Corporate Assets

10

Human Centred Knowledge Management

Knowledge management is about people. It's not about software, or documents or notes. It's about people who are the possessors of, and indicators to the location of knowledge in a company. It makes no sense to invent another knowledge management system which fails to take this really important factor into consideration. It is true that humans do not perform the knowledge management function in a company very well, but that's just because they are not omnipotent. If humans were omnipotent would we need to invent knowledge management systems? No, we wouldn't. So the goal of a knowledge management system should be to aim at making employees 'all knowing'.

Do You Know What You Know?

We have been deploying computer systems to perform a huge variety of functions in the company for several decades. The biggest failure of computer systems over the years has frequently been where systems were designed by people wanting to deploy a computer system rather than solve a problem. So the key to success lies in correct analysis of exactly what the knowledge management system is expected to do.

A good knowledge management system should simulate what a super well informed, well networked individual could do. A network of ultimate gatekeepers. So when starting out to deploy a knowledge management system it's best to look at the real knowledge resource in the company to see how that resource can best be used. What comprises the knowledge of people? Is it their know-how, their experience, their psychometric profile, their formal and informal education, the documents they have written or the projects they have worked on? The answer is yes. All of this comes together to make up the valuable knowledge of the individual.

KM Concept#38

Know What You Know

When you consider how much knowledge exists within a company it will never be possible to document it all so the answer is to develop a know-how base as the foundation for a knowledge management system. A know-how base is a knowledge base that knows where knowledge resides within the organization.

So let's consider exactly why we want a knowledge management system and what we expect it to be able to do. Below are some reasons a company might want to deploy a knowledge management system.

1 To know where particular expertise resides in the company.
2 To know what expertise is being lost when an employee leaves.
3 To know which individuals could perform a task as a team.
4 To understand how knowledge flows within the company.
5 To track competencies and proficiencies in the company.
6 To track the loss or acquisition of a particular competence or proficiency.

7 To locate documents and other media on particular topics.
8 To assist in planning for training.
9 To assist in planning for recruiting.
10 To access anecdotal material on customer accounts, problem solving, etc.

1 To Know Where Particular Expertise Resides in the Company

In order to know where particular expertise resides in the company you would need to know who knows what. That would mean performing an audit of competencies of individuals, job related knowledge, education and preferably proficiency. Competencies can be determined by looking at credentials such as the successful completion of training courses, academic qualifications and so forth. Proficiency is a measure of competence and experience and that's more difficult to characterize unless a mentoring scheme is in place which ensures that mentors are those who determine the level of proficiency of a particular individual based on his or her

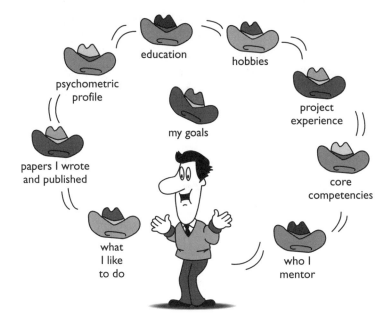

Figure 10.1 Profiling a person

competence and the job related knowledge which stems from expertise. If the goal is to determine where the expertise in the company resides then the answer to the question might be: 'Fred knows how to clean boilers', or a document which describes the process of how boilers are cleaned, or a file which contains information and data on boilers. In addition if job related knowledge is captured then anecdotal material on Fred's experiences of cleaning boilers could be captured in the system too.

Earlier we discussed expert systems. If the art of cleaning boilers was a dying art, or a rare resource which needs to be accessed in multiple locations there may be a need to build an expert system to advise an engineer on how to clean boilers. As an expert system is also a repository of knowledge the knowledge management system would need to lead the inquirer to the expert system as well.

2 To Know What Expertise is Being Lost When an Employee Leaves

It is extremely difficult to grasp exactly what a company is losing when an employee leaves, that is unless a knowledge management system is in place which has been tracking job related knowledge, competencies, proficiencies, education, work colleagues, etc. Properly designed, the knowledge management system should be able to track down the individuals who worked with the employee who has left the organization, so even if his or her expertise has been lost his colleagues might be able to assist in a crisis.

> **KM Concept#39**
>
> Knowledge Management Identifies Lost Expertise

3 To Know Which Individuals Could Perform a Task as a Team

Balancing teams is tough at the best of times. In a perfect world the team would comprise the best individuals from the perspective of proficiency, inter-personal skills, ability to work in a team, and would also include individuals with abilities such as analytic skills, leadership skills, or creative skills and so on. These aspects of the individual can be determined to a useful extent by the results of psychometric data.

4 To Understand How Knowledge Flows Within the Company

In order to understand how knowledge flows within an organization it is necessary to understand the formal and informal networking that exists inside and outside the company on a day to day basis. Understanding how particular employees learn and find out how to learn is key to understanding how knowledge flows within an organization. We have found that in a large organization, where you would expect a large number of gatekeepers, in a random selection of 25 individuals the same one or two names keep cropping up over and over again.

5 To Track Competencies and Proficiencies in the Company

Tracking competencies and proficiencies in a company is a bit like doing a stock take in a shop. These represent the key resources the organization has to work with in order to achieve its corporate goals. However tracking them in isolation from the other aspects of the individual is pointless. Just knowing that the organization has 28 gearbox design engineers, and 17 marketing executives is not useful. A richer picture is needed, the richness of the entire individual.

6 To Track the Loss or Acquisition of a Particular Competence or Proficiency

Organizations need to constantly reinvent themselves in order to keep up with the changing demands of industry. Take, for example, the Internet. Most organizations in the west have at least heard of the Internet, and many are beginning to use it as a marketing and sales vehicle for their products and services. As individuals learn about new technologies, the organization can determine its 'health' with respect to having the appropriate skills on board for the future. In the same way the KMS identifies the loss of expertise when an employee leaves.

7 To Locate Documents and Other Media on Particular Topics

It is so easy to recreate a document that someone else has already written, or redevelop a piece of software that has already been built by someone else. Once again, the key to knowing whether or not something has already been done is to look for identifiers. Identifiers for things which have been written are called authors. Authors are linked to documents by way of citing publications. There is no reason why this concept can't be extended to authors of anything. Software, videos, audio cassettes, marketing strategies, accounting procedures. If it has been recorded in whatever form, digital or paper, there is an author. Once again the human is the focal point.

8 To Assist in Planning for Training

How do human resource executives know what resources to grow in order to give companies access to the competencies, proficiencies, leadership, etc. that the organization needs to achieve its goals. First the organization needs to be able to characterize its goals. Next it needs to be able to identify critical knowledge functions which are required in order for those goals to be achieved. Next is the job of locating the optimal talent in the company that is best able to perform the task. At this point the HR executive ought to be able to determine whether or not the organization is sufficiently proficient to perform the task. Where it isn't, training is an option. Then of course there is the job of determining who is the best candidate for training and so on. This all sounds somewhat surreal I agree, but it is currently within the bounds of our knowledge and expertise to deploy such a system.

9 To Assist in Planning for Recruiting

If the time frame for training is not there, or there are no suitable candidates to be trained then the next option is to recruit a new member of staff from outside the company who already has the required expertise, proficiency and so on. When a new person joins the organization he or she usually joins to perform a specific function, and as such is introduced to the organization as 'the new engineer in charge of X', or the new marketing associate. A label is stuck on this person's forehead. His or her background is not observable to the new group of people who have never worked with this individual before, so therefore relevant and pertinent knowledge is lost to the organization, even though the company pays the individual for all of their know-how. A knowledge management system should catch such individuals as they join the company, building a profile on them to add to the knowledge management system.

10 To Access Anecdotal Material on Customer Accounts, Problem Solving, etc.

Job related knowledge by way of anecdotal material is valuable, and indeed organizations sometimes use groupware applications such as Lotus Notes to capture this type of information. The amount of time it takes to learn about a situation, be it a customer account, or a new piece of machinery, is investment in the individual on the part of the company. The investment may have no value to the individual out of context of a particular company, so when the individual leaves, the company actually loses twice. It loses because it paid for the employee to learn the information and it loses again because the information is lost completely when the individual leaves. How would it be possible for the company not to lose at all?

If the anecdotal material, and job related knowledge of the individual were captured and managed by a knowledge management system together with details of who the individual worked with on various projects the organization might hope not to lose so much. If the skill of the individual could be captured in some form of process document, the proficiency of the exiting individual would form the basis for growing competent individuals who could take his or her place. If the expertise were really rare, and codifiable, and the organization had already recognized in time that losing the expertise would mean that the organization was about to lose a significant asset, then plans could be made to build an expert system. The key issue for organizations is to understand what is of value and what is not.

┌─ KM Concept#40 ─────────────────────────────┐
│   │
│   Knowledge Management is About People   │
│   │
└──┘

Profiling a Person

The amount of data, information and knowledge that we could capture about an individual is of course enormous. So to begin with it is totally impractical to consider trying to do a comprehensive study of every employee in the company. So the best thing to do is to identify a part of the organization where improving access to knowledge would have a positive effect on the company very quickly. Examples include engineering organizations where individuals create new items and have to solve technical problems routinely. Another good example is groups of individuals who generate income through the 'sale' of knowledge and know-how, such as consultants. A third example is the part of the sales organization which deals with intelligence on customer accounts.

Having identified an area which looks as if performance could be improved due to improved knowledge sharing the next step is to determine exactly what type of knowledge would be of use. The example we discuss below is a rather generic situation where individuals in the organization are project oriented. The first part of the profile is the individual mission.

Mission

The purpose of the mission is to try to determine what it is about the individual that motivates him or her to work within the company. Examples of the mission for an individual might include: 'My mission is to ensure that ergonomics is taken into consideration with every piece of equipment my company designs'. Another example would be: 'My mission is to ensure that every product that leaves our factory has been acceptance tested to such and such a standard'. The mission tells you the context for the activity of the individual. It's often a secret too. We have discovered some raised eyebrows from our clients when they looked at what their employees perceived to be their mission.

Education

Education is pretty straight forward. Here we look at individuals since they were eighteen years old, that is entering tertiary education. Where individuals did not attend college we go back to when they left school. Here we are talking about formal education: courses, grades and so on. We would also include education which was job related. So perhaps an engineer would go on a course to learn how to maintain a 747, then exams would have to be passed. Perhaps an individual would go on a course to learn a new programming language like Java, but in this case maybe an exam wasn't taken as the course may have been given by a vendor rather than a formal academic body of some sort.

Job Related Knowledge

Job related knowledge looks at the informal lessons learnt as a result of participating in a particular project. If the project was to design a new undercarriage the types of things we would be interested in would be: What did you learn? What were the major obstacles? What would you do differently? Who did you work with? Who did you go to for specific types of help and so on? This activity can be as complex or simple as the context requires. We have successfully taken engineers back over a 25 year period, recording projects, collaborators, problems, co-workers. It's incredible that people remember so much: nicknames of co-workers from 20 years ago, disaster days and so forth. This activity is repeated over and over for every project until the current project is reached. The typical reaction to a long history over 20 years is usually amazement on all sides – management and the individual alike. It's so easy to forget how talented we all really are!

Hobbies

Hobbies are recorded as they reveal all sorts of secrets about the individual. I suppose it's obvious, but people pursue hobbies because they have an interest or skill they like to use which they don't have an opportunity to use in the workplace. Perhaps the most notable example I recall was a lady who was a world expert in cockpit ergonomics whose hobby was trans-European classic car rallying. This lady not only participated, she planned and ran rallies. So in addition to her formidable knowledge of ergonomics she was also a logistics expert. This type of knowledge about the individual is of interest to the company.

Competencies and Proficiencies

In this section we look to characterize competencies primarily and deal with proficiency afterwards.

We are looking to identify a minimum of four competencies for a person in their early twenties, and perhaps eight for a more mature individual. We have spent an awful lot of time wondering about the possible impact on a system of a person pretending to be more competent than they really are. In fact it was our clients who convinced us that the system as a whole would be self-regulating as individuals would be putting themselves at huge risk if they claimed to be expert boiler fitters, when in fact they were really only at apprentice level. So here we start by letting individuals claim a competence. That may later be revised if their perception of the scale of competence is different to that of a more experienced person. We did find that generally younger employees claim to be more competent than their more mature colleagues think they are!

This situation can be avoided if the baseline for a competence is documented. One example of this could be the NVQ system which is used in the UK. Ideally competence levels for all jobs should be identified and documented so there is no argument as to whether an individual is as competent as he or she claims. This would be a huge task for a company to mount, and we do not believe that it is necessary to do this in order to launch a useful system.

Psychometrics

There is a wealth of information that could be used in this section. It also has the potential to be a minefield. We have found that the vast majority have no objection to some psychometric indicators being shown in a public system. The one which seems to be most acceptable is Briggs–Myers. Psychometrics which portray a picture of whether a person is extrovert/ introvert, intuitive/perceptive and so forth have so far not seemed to be too intrusive. Other indicators concerning leadership and team skills would also be of use as open knowledge in the company. There are however many psychometric tests which would not be suitable for public access within the organization. As always it depends on the context within which the system is expected to perform.

At this point it is worth saying that the systems we have designed so far have all been designed to be 'open'. That means that everyone in the organization can access not only their own record but everyone else's as well. If we were to propose a system where only management or human resources had access to records we do not anticipate that participants would be anything like as open as we have always found.

Professional

The term professional refers to how the individual looks to the outside world. What organizations do they belong to? What papers or books have they written? Do they teach at any organizations outside the company? Have they filed any patents?

So here we have a nice building block, a template if you like, to look at certain types of individuals. Context is everything, and what we are interested in is ensuring that the information, knowledge and data that is captured about the individual is appropriate and right for the application for which it was designed.

GETTING STARTED

You may recall that earlier in this book we spoke about interviews and knowledge elicitation. Well this is where it comes into use. Below is a sample list of the types of questions an interviewer may wish to use in building a profile much as it has been described here. One important question is time. How long does this process take? For an average employee a record can be constructed in approximately 2–3 hours. Yes, that's a long time. So the risk/reward of setting up such as system has to be investigated before such an initiative is launched. But we always do that as a matter of course, don't we?

QUESTIONS FOR A KNOW-HOW AUDIT

Can you give me a summary of your education?
Where/what was your first job?
What competencies did it involve?
Can we break that down into something more specific?
You say you worked in _____, can you characterize that for me?
Do you think you needed _____ experience for that job/task?
Wouldn't that be quite hard without _____?
Would that be all/enough for that job?
How long did you work in that job?
Can we stick a name on that job/project?

So where are we now? What was your next job?
Can we summarize that as _____?

And now we're at your current job?
Have we gone through all your projects?

When you get involved in projects . . . are you a visionary or a hands on?
In a team situation what role do you take on?
Are you competitive?

Have you done any psychometric tests? Briggs–Myers?
Do you know what sort of problem solving profile you have?
Would you mind perhaps doing one?

This is a polar diagram. Let's say this is your job and these are the things you need to do your job, what are these things? And these circles represent levels of skill; 5 is the best in your company and 1 is an innocent. Can we draw you in? How do you rank yourself as a . . . ? A . . . ? A . . . ?

Do you think your colleagues could identify you from this polar diagram? If we were to use this model, could you identify the different levels? Could you classify your peers on this polar diagram?

Imagine a special project came along that you really wanted to do/that they really needed you for, but it was based in Australia for 2 years. And so you have to find someone to do your job for 2 years. That is, someone would need to do your job not forever, not long enough to build up a lot of experience in it. What would that person need to be able to do? If you could say they needed to be able to blah and blah and blah, what would those things be?

If we tried to characterize what you can do, for example if you said 'if you need _____ and if you need _____ and if you need _____ , then call me', what would those three things be?

Can you tell me what you're good at? What you're bad at? What you like and what you don't like?

If you have an intractable problem, if there's something you're completely stuck on, where would you go? What would you do? Who would you go to for help?

Do you use the Web?
Would you if it was available at your desk?

Tell me a little about your aspirations. What are your career goals?

What are your hobbies?
What haven't we asked you that you expected to be asked?
What haven't we asked you that you think we should have asked you?
Can we have your phone number and job title? Do you have a business card?

You can see that the questions are aimed at keeping a dialogue moving between interviewer and interviewee.

11

Guarding and Growing the Corporate Memory

First let's go back to the bigger picture of intellectual capital and look at the processes which enable us to guard our intangible assets. We will start with market centred assets. The process with which we look after assets which give the company power in the marketplace is called market strategy. This is the activity which ensures that we get maximum leverage from our brands, loyal customers, distribution channels and so forth. Intellectual property management is the business process which ensures that our intellectual property is protected by patent, copyright, etc. Theoretically it also ensures that our intellectual property is properly leveraged: that would include licensing, measures of return on investment and so on. Very few companies actually practise good intellectual property management. Infrastructure assets are managed by organization and methods, yet these practices rarely take management philosophy or corporate culture into consideration, so the business process has to be either expanded or reinvented.

┌─ KM Concept#41 ──

Knowledge Management is a Part of Intellectual Capital Management

└──

Finally knowledge management is the process by which we manage human centred assets. Notice the difference between the human resource function which also concerns itself with the management of people in the workplace. Also knowledge management is not the same as intellectual capital. Many people have confused the two for some reason, but the word, 'management', in knowledge management definitely suggests a process, whereas intellectual capital is an entity, an asset, not a process. So the function of knowledge management is to guard and grow knowledge owned by individuals, and where possible, transfer the asset into a form where it can be more readily shared by other employees in the company.

Corporate memory is comprised of the knowledge management system, documents, videos and so forth. It also helps us access other IT systems such as expert and knowledge based systems. Together they assist us in managing a wide variety of knowledge about employees, customers and various aspects of the operation of the business. The corporate memory is an infrastructure asset which has to be guarded and grown over a long period of time. It's interesting to speculate on the monetary value of corporate memory. We know that in recent years there has been an increasing trend for the percentage of a company's net worth to be biased

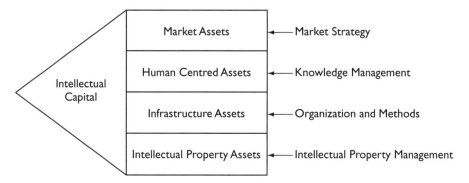

Figure 11.1 Intellectual capital management processes

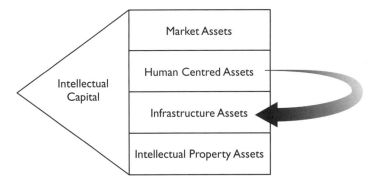

Figure 11.2 Knowledge management turns human centred assets into infrastructure assets

towards intangible rather than tangible assets. If a company had a tangible memory this would move some of the 'mystery' from intangible assets. As such, its use, and impact on the organization, forms a valuable part of Intellectual Capital. So in the future we can expect one of the motives for the acquisition of a company to be the acquisition of its corporate memory.

From a legal perspective a KMS can be protected by copyright, as all software can be. However its true value is not so much the value of the written word, more in how it is applied in the context of the business activity. Just because a corporate memory exists does not mean it is put to optimal use by the organization.

WHOSE BABY IS THE CORPORATE MEMORY?

There is a nasty risk that some organizations will fail to get real benefit from the existence of a corporate memory because of territorial wars over its ownership. We have already seen memos in one client site where the HR department directed the consulting group to 'keep its hands off' knowledge management because it 'belonged to them'. This is a really good way to kill the initiative, which is exactly what happened in this instance. There are important guarding tasks of the memory with respect to backing up files which contain information and knowledge about each employee, and that is an IT systems function, so it should be performed by the IT department. The systems themselves will need to be built, maintained and updated, and that is also an IT systems function. In terms of 'ownership' there is really nothing to fight about, provided access is given to people that need it as and when they need it. Ownership is not an issue if everybody has the ability to do what they need to do.

SECURITY

This is a really substantial issue, as contained within the KMS there may be huge quantities of very sensitive information and knowledge. Therefore access systems and perhaps a hierarchy of security may need to be put in place. Imagine a scenario where a new product is being developed. It would be foolish to enable all employees in the organization to have access to information on the new product; before long competitors would know the company's secret plans. Yet security in such circumstances is not a new concept, as we already deal with security in our company. So it makes sense to establish security systems which mirror how employees would be expected to behave in real life.

Passwords

Access to the KMS should be password protected in much the same ways as we protect others from reading our e-mail. Certain parts of records may be accessible to everyone in the company, other parts may be too sensitive for all employees to have access to. It all depends on the company, its business and how employees feel about the system.

CONCURRENCY AND ACCESS

Some KMS are going to grow to be huge systems. They will require large servers upon which the system will keep the growing employee records. Consider a situation where a company has offices in different parts of the world. One systems option would be to have a 'memory' in each office, another would be to have a central repository somewhere. Again none of these issues are either new or unsolvable as the IT industry has had to solve such problems before wherever databases are distributed. The most important factor here is to ensure that the knowledge contained within the system has integrity, that is that it is accurate at all times.

CORPORATE MEMORY AS A PRODUCT OR SERVICE?

If an organization has documented its knowledge in a KMS it stands to reason that there may be a new business opportunity for the company based on selling access to its corporate memory. If a company specialized in putting out oil well fires, it might discover that over a period of time anecdotal material, advice, case histories, snippets of knowledge from grand masters and tried and tested procedures were of interest to other companies, in this case oil companies. There is money to be made by selling access to parts of the corporate memory. Like all new business opportunities this has to be evaluated to ensure that the crown jewels are not given away, but we anticipate that this will form the basis for new businesses in the next millennium.

EXTENDING THE CORPORATE NETWORK

The KMS can be opened up to external companies that are associated with the organization. It might be desirable to extend the network to manufacturers of the company's products, suppliers and distributors. This notion is synergistic with the concept of the virtual company. Where are the boundaries of the company? The answer for the future is 'Wherever we decide to put them'.

The Knowledge Management Officer

This is a new job title which some companies have decided to introduce in order to have a person who is responsible for the implementation of KMS, or even to be the guardian of knowledge in the organization. This is a curious step, and perhaps reflects a reticence to redefine job functions that are already there. To establish a knowledge management officer as a means of promoting knowledge management in the organization may be an interesting early step. Such a person may be an evangelist for the knowledge management philosophy in the company. But no one person can be responsible for ensuring knowledge management in an organization. It has to be embraced by the entire company, all employees taking responsibility for their own part in the process. In third millennium

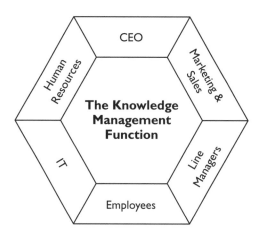

Figure 11.3 The knowledge management function

companies several existing corporate functions will need to be redefined and then work together to guard the corporate memory.

The Role of the CEO

The role of the CEO is to set the stage for a culture which embodies, and most of all values all aspects of knowledge sharing in the organization. Without this key role being satisfied the prognosis for the long-term growth of a corporate memory is poor.

> ┌─ KM Concept#42 ─────────────────────
> │
> │   Knowledge Sharing Makes Everyone Powerful
> │

The Role of Human Resources

One of the functions of human resources is to ensure that the organization has access to proficient staff now and in the future. In order to satisfy this goal the human resource function has to be seen as strategic. As such they are concerned with both guarding current human resources, and growing new resources either organically or inorganically. None of these activities can be performed in isolation from the rest of the knowledge management function.

The Role of Line Managers

Line managers are responsible for the smooth operation of various projects, business units, etc. Their role in supporting the knowledge management function is twofold. First they need to reinforce the policy of using knowledge management by checking that their projects and staff do not reinvent the wheel. Second they need to ensure that their staff use the knowledge management system as a repository for new knowledge, lessons learnt and so forth.

The Role of Information Technology Managers

Like all IT systems the knowledge management system needs to be fit for purpose. Ensuring that it is, is the job of the IT manager. This requirement is a design requirement which needs to be assured before any system is specified, built, bought and deployed. Once the system has been deployed, ensuring that it is kept secure, current, etc. is the job of the IT department, just as protecting and maintaining any IT system or database.

The Marketing and Sales Roles

Knowledge of markets is the key to competitive advantage for many companies. Yet knowledge of markets, customers and so forth is easily lost and not distributed effectively enough for all employees to respond appropriately when a customer phones the company. It is in the best interests of the company that marketing and sales function efficiently to take active steps to guard, grow and disseminate knowledge concerning marketing and sales. To have such knowledge made available to any employee who might come into contact with a customer is so important that we have split this function from other operating functions. Fragmented knowledge concerning markets will not be of use to the general employee, knowledge which has been organized so that a wide variety of individuals in the company can use it is more desirable.

The Role of the Employees

The role of the employees in the knowledge management function is to use the system, update records that they are responsible for, and ensure that their own input is of high quality and integrity. Remember: garbage in garbage out.

LINKING TO EXISTING SYSTEMS

When an organization decides to embody a knowledge sharing philosophy, they are probably not starting with a blank sheet of paper, unless the company is brand new, of course. There will be masses of resources already in the company that need to be brought into the system. The most obvious examples are documents. The logical way to do this is to link documents to the know-how base by way of their author. Please note that we are not talking about knowledge management systems performing document management, for that's not the case. We are talking about establishing a link whereby documents which have been written can be located and accessed by others if necessary. We are not proposing a mammoth effort where every document that the company ever had is microfiched, or digitized, although that would be nice; the first step is just to remember that they exist and provide a mechanism for locating them. So if a document happens to be in a filing cabinet that is all well and good.

LAST WORDS ON GUARDING AND GROWING THE CORPORATE MEMORY

The corporate memory is potentially the greatest asset any company could ever generate in their life. Today it is difficult to foresee exactly how large these systems will become or how valuable they will be in terms of dollars. One thing for sure is that they will be big, and valuable. When thinking about the growth and guardianship of the corporate memory I dearly wish I could just say, well that's the job of the knowledge management officer, but it's not. That would be like saying that looking after the company's reputation is the job of public relations, or that quality was the job of the person who established the ISO procedures. In fact the job of protecting the company's reputation is every employee's responsibility, and so is quality.

Guarding and growing the corporate memory is also the responsibility of every employee, because without that commitment, it's not a corporate memory, it's a partial memory.

12

What to Do on Monday Morning

So here we are, it's Monday morning and you are filled with bright ideas concerning knowledge management. You have concluded that your company can benefit from adopting a knowledge sharing philosophy and by having an infrastructure that supports it. Where do you start?

The first thing to do is to determine how management feel about the idea of knowledge sharing. If it is at all possible to have the CEO as the champion of knowledge management then that is highly desirable. Maybe you will have to put together a seminar of knowledge management especially for the management team, then provide a forum for management to discuss the impact it would have on various projects.

THE INTRODUCTORY SEMINAR

In our experience an introductory seminar is a great way to kick off a knowledge management initiative. The first task is to decide who to invite. As we have already stated if you can get the CEO to attend, that's great. If they are not available try for the COO and operating managers whose day to day efficiency will be directly impacted by availability and access to the right knowledge at the right place at the right time. Project leaders are good invitees, especially if the company generates revenue by selling project expertise. Examples would include consulting companies, legal firms and so forth. Two other good invitees are the VP of Sales and VP of Marketing. As we have already discussed market knowledge and its availability to sales persons and product developers is extremely important, and usually not well provided for. Account knowledge which could be shared between sales people whilst they are in the company, is also a valuable long-term asset which provides continuity long after they have left.

The Content of the Seminar

The invitees to the seminar are all busy people, so the event should not be planned to last for more than three hours. That doesn't mean that three hours will be long enough, it won't, but if you plan for it to be longer you may find that people don't turn up because they think it is too much time to spend. There is time to correctly position the importance of knowledge management later. This event is just a taste of what's to come. The ideal agenda is one where there is some thought provoking material presented for about an hour and a half, then at least an hour to discuss the importance of knowledge management within your particular company. Finally leave some time at the end to develop an action plan. Mornings are best; start at nine, and then by adding a working lunch an extra hour can be stolen.

Sample Agenda

9.00   Introduction to knowledge management (types of knowledge, tacit is explicit knowledge, automatic knowledge, goal setting knowledge, systematic knowledge)

10.00   Critical knowledge functions, how knowledge is created in the enterprise, sources and sinks of knowledge

11.00 Break
11.15 Brainstorm
12.15 Working lunch and development of action plan

Brainstorm

Put together a brainstorming session which looks at the impact knowledge sharing might have in your organization. However, when putting a brainstorm together make sure it is properly managed, perhaps using de Bono's six thinking hats method. This will stop someone who is very negative blowing your cause out of the window in the first ten seconds. There is bound to be someone in the audience who will ask what the cost of deploying a knowledge management system in the company will be. Sadly, we can't answer that question in terms of man days that need to be spent just yet, so look for situations where having a knowledge management solution would have saved the company time and money.

The brainstorming session might be managed in some part by looking at some of the following issues:

1 What is critical knowledge in your company?
2 How do people that need it know where to locate it?
3 Is the knowledge codified in any way?
4 Can it be codified?
5 Does the knowledge only reside in certain people's heads?
6 How easy is it to transfer from one person to another?
7 How common or rare is the knowledge?
8 How would widespread access to this knowledge affect the organization?
9 What would happen if 'keepers' of this knowledge left the company?
10 How can the company protect itself against certain types of knowledge loss?
11 What type of knowledge does the company need to achieve its corporate goals?
12 What kinds of knowledge does the company need to achieve its 3 or 5 year plan?
13 How will the company ensure that it has the right knowledge in the right place at the right time?

There are some fairly juicy agenda items here, so there is no worry that the brainstorm will run out of things to discuss. Pick two or three items from the above list to kick things off. One favourite is to look at a recent project which was not as successful as it should have been, and see whether access to knowledge played any part in its sub-optimal performance.

The Action Plan

The potential knowledge management function in any company is huge, so an initial attempt to provide a total solution would be a mistake. At the beginning, pick a target group who could benefit from knowledge sharing as people. Forget computer solutions, just stick to people. Bring together a working group to become evangelists of knowledge management within the company. If the company is large and distributed over many sites use the Internet as a communications mechanism. Pick a particular individual or team which has critical knowledge that a wider audience could benefit from having access to. Determine how best that knowledge could be shared within the organization. Look at critical processes in the company and see who understands how to use those processes and who understands how and why they work. If a brown bag lunch seminar is the first step that's fine. This may well turn out to be a cultural issue in your company.

SOME OTHER IDEAS FOR ACTIONS

Action 1

Prepare a list of projects for which you are responsible. Then for each project write five lines on three potential outcomes.

Outcome 1 – The project is a show stopper – a huge success.
Outcome 2 – The project is mediocre.
Outcome 3 – The project is a disaster.

This task should help to prioritize projects, so then it might be worth looking at the relative resources assigned to various projects.

Action 2

Now for each 'important' project, develop a Dream Ticket as outlined in Chapter 2. Organize elements of the project under the headings: Market Assets, Intellectual Property Assets, Infrastructure Assets and Human Centred Assets. Grow the list as long as you can. If you are a CEO or an operating manager the list typically turns out to be around 25–30 elements organized under each of the categories. If you have line responsibility for an aspect of a product or service, your list may be smaller and biased to your own expertise. That's alright, just ask a colleague whose expertise is complimentary to help flesh out the other areas. Better still brainstorm the dream ticket with a multi-talented team.

Action 3

Look at the area of human centred assets; in particular look for expertise which represents a high risk factor to the project. That's to say, if the knowledge were not available for one reason or another (getting run over by a truck), the project could fail. Assume the worst. Think about a backup plan, how difficult would that be to adopt? How quickly could it be done and how much would it cost?

DON'T GO OUT AND BUY COMPUTER SOFTWARE

The temptation to go out and try to buy something on the market which will provide an infrastructure for corporate knowledge management will be very tempting. Resist. At this time there is no offering on the market which is able to provide appropriate infrastructure for corporate knowledge management. IT companies are already relabelling their information technology solutions as knowledge management solutions, as will some of the document management companies. But neither of these solutions reflect the true infrastructure of knowledge in the company – people. But don't lose heart, all is not lost, there will be a solution on the market soon, keep in touch!

Sources, Sinks and Guardians

In his book, *In Search of Excellence,* Tom Peters referred to 'walking around' as a style of management. Indeed it is a good idea to wander around the company and see if you can identify sources, sinks and gatekeepers. Introduce the terminology to your colleagues, There are of course more formal methods which we use in a consulting scenario, but an informal approach should be very useful to begin with. See if you can tell where ideas get stuck in a company or department. See if you can identify places where knowledge or innovation gets killed which are inappropriate. Look for informal groups who share knowledge in the company and see how effective they are. Who lunches together? Who has coffee together? Who smokes or drinks together? Who runs together at lunchtime or plays racquetball together?

If you are a manager, look at the location of your office in the company. Once when I was Director of a research group years ago, we moved into new offices and as I was just about to pick the plum office in the building, my boss stopped me and pointed out that that no one would have to walk past my office at any time, as it was at the end of the corridor. Instead he advised me to choose an office which was in between the kitchen and bathroom. Everyone had to walk past my office several times a day. In that way it was possible to get a feeling of who visited who in which office.

Ask people who they go to when they have a problem. Categorize problems. Keep track of the answers. You will be surprised how much you can learn in a couple of days.

Look for Critical Knowledge Functions

There will be places in the company where there is a greater reliance on knowledge than there is in other places. These can be located by asking around to see if there is a scarce knowledge resource for any particularly important corporate function. How many people know how to reload the e-mail system? How many people know how to set up some machinery on the factory floor? How many people know how to fix a particular piece of machinery? By identifying scarce resources it is then possible to speculate on how critical the loss of that person would be to the company. Are there fiefdoms in your company where knowledge is jealously guarded? Do these fiefdoms work to the general good of the company, or otherwise?

What if No One Knows What's Critical?

You may find yourself in the tricky situation where you can't get to the root of the issue as people will say things like, 'Well what's critical and what isn't depends upon what's happening that day'. This may be the case, especially when an organization is fighting for its life. We'll talk about that in a minute. But if the management group can't agree on what is critical and what isn't this is an indication that the company has lost its way. The solution here is to go back to the beginning of this book and look at the construction of a dream ticket, or hierarchies of them as appropriate. If there is not enough information contained in this book, there is a forthcoming book in my Intellectual Capital Series, which is dedicated to the subject, entitled *Dream Ticket – Corporate Strategy with Intangible Assets*, which gives a lot more information on how to focus the organization, and plan to grow intangible assets, which include knowledge.

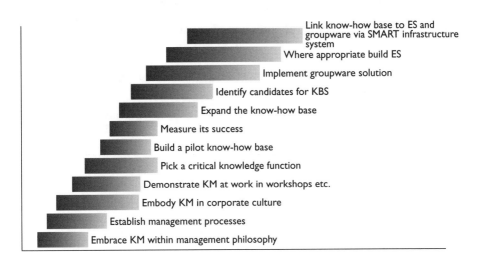

Figure 12.1 Planning for knowledge management

YESTERDAY, TODAY AND TOMORROW

Last year we performed an intellectual capital audit in an organization, part of which looked at critical knowledge functions. Critical knowledge was identified to be associated mostly with three individuals who played two roles in the company. One was pre-sales technical support, the other post-sales customer support. The other critical knowledge in the company was related to the manufacturing process. This is interesting as just six people out of 40 possessed the critical operating knowledge which sustained the company, three of which were tied to almost every sale in either the front or back end of the process. Further, the sales process was extremely long and complex, over three or four years, so these individuals should have been spending all of their time on new business instead of dealing with customer complaints. As it was the same three people who supported both the front and back end part of the sales process, new sales were in fact competing with existing customers, a situation which can cause a company to get stuck if existing customers have lots of complaints. This is exactly what had happened, the company had had problems achieving its targets for several years. We decided to analyse how a number of key individuals spent their time in terms of:

1. activities which would result in tomorrow's business;
2. activities which would result in closing today's business;
3. activities relating to sales that were made yesterday, and beyond.

On average the individuals questioned came up with the following numbers:

1. activities which would result in tomorrow's business = 10 per cent of time;
2. activities which would result in closing today's business = 20 per cent of time;
3. activities relating to sales that were made yesterday, and beyond = 70 per cent of time.

In fact, these three individuals, the only three in the company able to provide pre-sales support, were spending the majority of their time with customers who were in fact unhappy with the product they had already bought.

In this organization, even though the critical knowledge was associated with customer support, the real problem was unhappy customers. Why were they unhappy? They were unhappy because the product was of inconsistent quality. So critical knowledge was also associated with improving the predictability of the manufacturing process. Fix that and the sales team could focus on new sales, then the company would have a better chance of achieving increased sales.

So it's important not to get confused by the 'noise', and get to the real issue at hand.

Too Busy to Do My Job

Another interesting exercise is to look at exactly what individuals do. If someone has the function of controller, what exactly do they spend their time doing? If they are also involved in customer care, maybe it's an indication that something is amiss. In another organization we have worked with it seemed that everyone had their fingers into at least three pies. Everyone was always too busy to do their own job as they were 'helping someone else out'. They in turn were being 'helped out'. They were also producing reports no one read, creating multiple databases, all sorts of things, which did not focus on contributing to the functions of the core business. They needed help to refocus and reorganize.

Beware of Re-engineering Expertise out of the Organization

In such circumstances organizations may decide to re-engineer. This can be a very positive process, provided the exercise does not engineer valuable knowledge out of the company. So if an individual looks like he or she does not have a clear role in the company, or perhaps no line responsibility, before making the person redundant have a good look to see what he or she really does and exactly what he or she knows. To make redundant a gatekeeper is a really bad move. To let valuable knowledge walk out of the door is the same as setting fire to a pile of money. Just make sure you know what the organization is losing when every single employee leaves, voluntarily or otherwise.

SKUNK WORKS

Finally it is sometimes necessary to demonstrate success before you can get permission to have a project. If that's the case in your company, it's hard luck, but you just might have to go ahead and start an initiative as a skunk works project. It's sometimes easier to ask for forgiveness than permission.

Good Luck!

┌─ KM Concept#43 ──────────────────────────┐

Corporate Memories May Live Forever

Summary of KM Concepts

#1 – Knowledge = Information in Context + Understanding
#2 – Knowledge is Underutilized in the Organization
#3 – Knowledge Adds Value to Products and Services
#4 – Knowledge Provides Competitive Advantage
#5 – Knowledge of Markets is a Business Weapon
#6 – Knowledge is the Basis for Creating Intellectual Property
#7 – Knowledge, Like People, is Transient
#8 – Dream Tickets Give Us Knowledge to Achieve Goals
#9 – Identify Critical Knowledge Functions
#10 – Know Who Knows What in the Company
#11 – Knowledge About Customers Makes Selling Easier
#12 – Knowledge About People Means Better Teams
#13 – Job Titles Mask Knowledge About People
#14 – Proficient People are Competent and have Experience
#15 – Organizational Capability = Competence + Proficiency

#16 – Making Knowledge Explicit Generates Infrastructure Assets
#17 – Goal Setting Knowledge Creates Dream Tickets
#18 – Strive to Make Critical Knowledge Explicit
#19 – Know Why Knowledge is Tacit
#20 – Know Where Deep Knowledge Needs to be Captured
#21 – Know How to Elicit Knowledge
#22 – Know What Modality Knowledge Will Be Used For
#23 – Know How Dynamic Knowledge Is
#24 – Know Who Needs to Know What in the Organization
#25 – Use Expert Systems to Capture Deep Knowledge
#26 – Understand How Knowledge is Generated
#27 – Knowledge is Fluid – Know How it Flows
#28 – Know Who are the Sources and Sinks of Knowledge
#29 – Know the Whereabouts of Knowledge Networks
#30 – Corporate Culture Must Support Knowledge Sharing
#31 – Corporate Heroes Share Knowledge
#32 – All Employees Have Knowledge About Corporate Goals
#33 – Knowledge Sharing is the Way We Do Things Around Here
#34 – Knowledge Management Supports Human Resource Planning
#35 – Management Processes Deliver Knowledge Management
#36 – Knowledge Sharing is Part of our Corporate Culture
#37 – KMS Infrastructures are Corporate Assets
#38 – Know What You Know
#39 – Knowledge Management Identifies Lost Expertise
#40 – Knowledge Management is About People
#41 – Knowledge Management is a Part of Intellectual Capital Management
#42 – Knowledge Sharing Makes Everyone Powerful
#43 – Corporate Memories May Live Forever

References and

Further Reading

Block, P. (1987) *The Empowered Manager*, Jossey-Bass Inc.

Brooking, A. (1996) *Intellectual Capital: Core Asset for the Third Millenium Enterprise*, International Thomson Business Press.

David, R. and Lenat, D. (1982) *Knowledge Based Systems in Artificial Intelligence*, McGraw-Hill Inc.

Deal, T. and Kennedy, A. (1982) *Corporate Culture*, Addison-Wesley Publishing Company Inc.

Ericsson, K.A. and Simon, H.E. (1984) *Protocol Analysis Verbal Reports as Data*, The Massachusetts Institute of Technology Press.

Forsyth, R. (1984) *Expert Systems Principles and Case Studies*, Chapman and Hall Ltd.

Leonard-Barton, D. (1995) *Wellsprings of Knowledge*, Harvard Business School Press.

Lorriman, J. and Young, R. (1995) *Upside Down Management*, McGraw-Hill International (UK) Limited.

McCorduck, P. (1979) *Machines Who Think*, W. H. Freeman and Company.

Negroponte, N. (1995) *Being Digital*, Hodder and Stoughton.

Nonaka, I. and Takeuchi, H. (1995) *The Knowledge Creating Company*, Oxford University Press.

Peters, T.J. and Waterman, R.H., Jr (1982) *In Search of Excellence: Lessons from America's Best-run Companies*, New York: Harper.

Pheysey, D. (1993) *Organizational Cultures*, Routledge.

Rust, J. and Golombok, S. (1989) *Modern Psychometrics*, Routledge.

Stewart, T. (1997) *Intellectual Capital*, Nicholas Brealey Publishing.

Sveiby, K.E. (1997) *The New Organizational Wealth*, Berrett-Koehler Publishers Inc.

Wielinga, B., Boose, J., Gaines, B., Schrieber, G. and Van Someren, M. (1990) *Current Trends in Knowledge Acquisition*, IOS Press.

Wiig, K. (1993) *Knowledge Management Foundations*, Schema Press Ltd.

Wiig, K. (1994) *Knowledge Management*, Schema Press Ltd.

Wiig, K. (1995) *Knowledge Management Methods*, Schema Press Ltd.

Winston, P.H. (1984) *Artificial Intelligence*, Addison-Wesley Publishing Company Inc.

INDEX

About the Author

Annie Brooking, Managing Director and founder of The Technology Broker, has worked in the high technology industry for 26 years. She is recognized in the areas of tactical and strategic marketing, management, strategic planning, technology and the emerging areas of Intellectual Capital and Knowledge Management. She has held management and executive positions at Sun Microsystems Inc. and Symbolics Inc. where she directed the marketing group and was responsible for the successful negotiation of multi-million dollar strategic alliances. She has had extensive international consulting experience with start-up corporations on both management and technical issues.

Brooking founded and managed Europe's first industrial Artificial Intelligence research and consulting group, The Knowledge Based Systems Centre in the United Kingdom. She has served as a consultant to the European Economic Community in Brussels on advanced information processing for 14 years. In addition, in 1983 she designed the first successful advanced information processing project for the CEC's project ESPRIT, a methodology for the design of knowledge based systems.

Brooking has lectured widely both publicly and in academic institutions on numerous topics related to computer science and high technology. During her early career she worked as an academic, holding a variety of posts at South Bank and Brunel Universities. She is co-author of two books on Artificial Intelligence, and one on Managing Technology. In 1996 she wrote the first book to be published on Intellectual Capital.

Brooking's extensive expertise and contracts throughout the world give her an insight into how industry can best use technologies for profit. She has completed post-graduate studies in computer science at Brunel University in the UK.

Brooking has lived in the UK, Malta, Australia and the US. She now lives in Cambridge, UK.

Annie Brooking can be contacted at The Technology Broker on:
Phone: +441–954–261199
FAX: +441–954–260291
e-mail: annie@tbroker.co.uk